PowerPoint

Making the most of
Microsoft® PowerPoint

Works

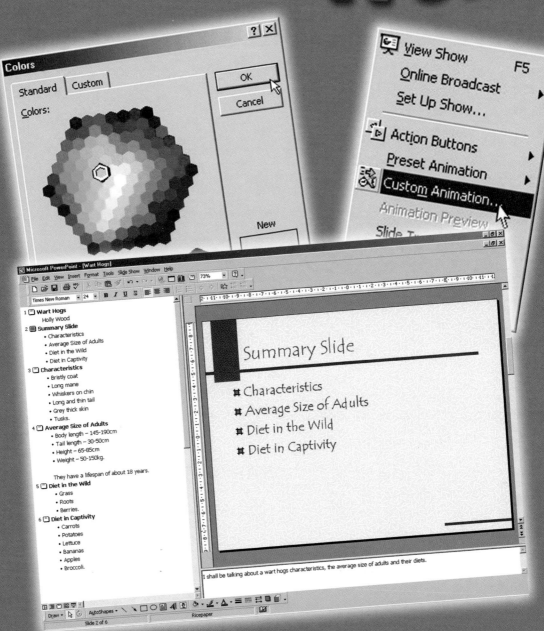

FOLENS

Patricia Harrison   **Papia Sarkar**

Dear Reader,

ICT is changing everyone's lives. At work, in the home and in school, what we do and how we do it has been transformed by the use of computers. The most widely used presentation package around the world is Microsoft® **PowerPoint**. In writing this book, we have taken the 53 most important functions of **PowerPoint**, which will be of help to you in your work in school.

Each left-hand page takes you step-by-step through a single function. The screenshots help you to recognise on your screen what you are seeing on the page. These pages are called **skill** pages and can be used to learn the skill and to refer back to, whatever you are doing, to remind yourself of how to carry out a function.

Skills are useful only if you can use them to improve your work. Each right-hand page therefore provides an opportunity to apply your skill in a practical context. These are called **Application** pages. Once you have learned and applied a skill, you should look for opportunities in your school work to apply this skill regularly. In this way, it will become second nature to you. Your work will improve across the whole curriculum and particularly in your ability to **communicate** effectively.

Enjoy the book and be confident that, if you learn from it, your attainment and self-confidence will increase.

Best wishes

Patricia Papia

Contents

Creating a Title Slide

1a

SKILL

When you open *PowerPoint*, this **Dialog Box** will appear.

1 Click **Blank Presentation**.

2 Click **OK**.

3 Click **Title Slide** from the **AutoLayout** options.

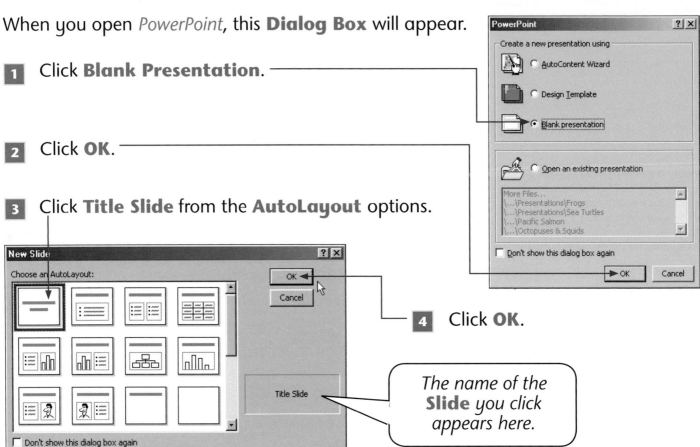

4 Click **OK**.

*The name of the **Slide** you click appears here.*

5 Click the first **Text Box** and type the title of your presentation.

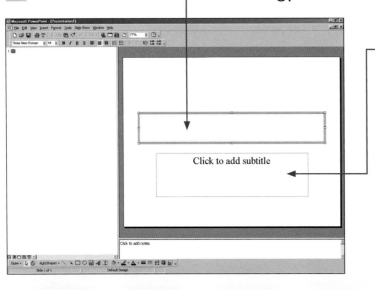

6 Click the second **Text Box** and type the subtitle.

7 Click anywhere on the screen and the **Text Box** outlines will disappear.
The first **Slide** of your presentation is now complete.

PowerPointWorks

About Me

You are going to create a presentation called 'About Me'.

1 Create a **Title Slide**. (See 1a)

2 Type the title of the presentation.

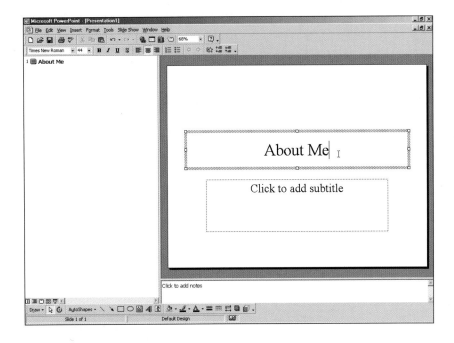

*The number of the slide and the text that is on it appears here, in the **Outline Pane**.*

3 Type your full name in the subtitle box.

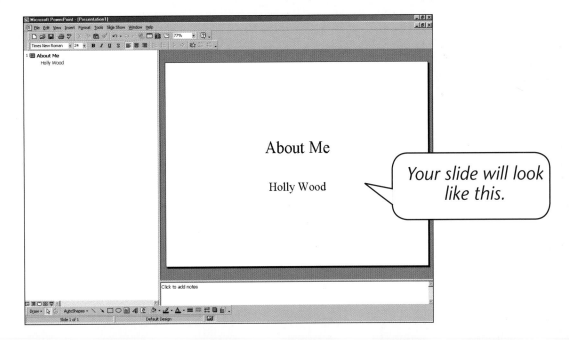

4 **Save**.

Your slide will look like this.

2a

SKILL

Opening an Existing Presentation and Editing Text

Opening an existing presentation

1 Click **File**.

2 Click **Open**.

3 Click the File you want to **Open**.

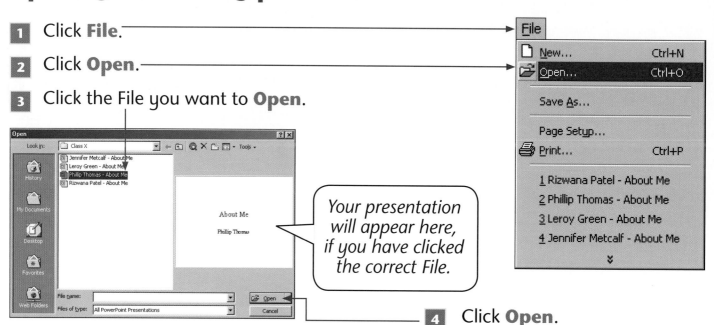

Your presentation will appear here, if you have clicked the correct File.

4 Click **Open**.

Editing text

5 Click the **Text Box** you want to **Edit**.

6 Move the cursor to where you want to insert or delete text.

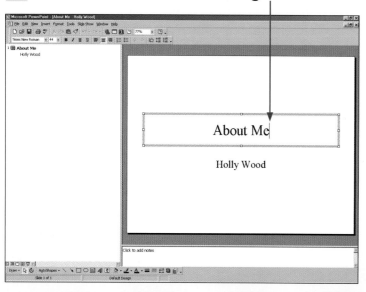

7 Type your new text or change the text.

*To replace all the text in the **Text Box**, highlight the text and type your new text.*

1 **Open** your 'About Me' presentation. (See 2a)

2 Change the title to 'My Best Friend'.

*You can create a new presentation by **Opening** and **Editing** an existing presentation.*

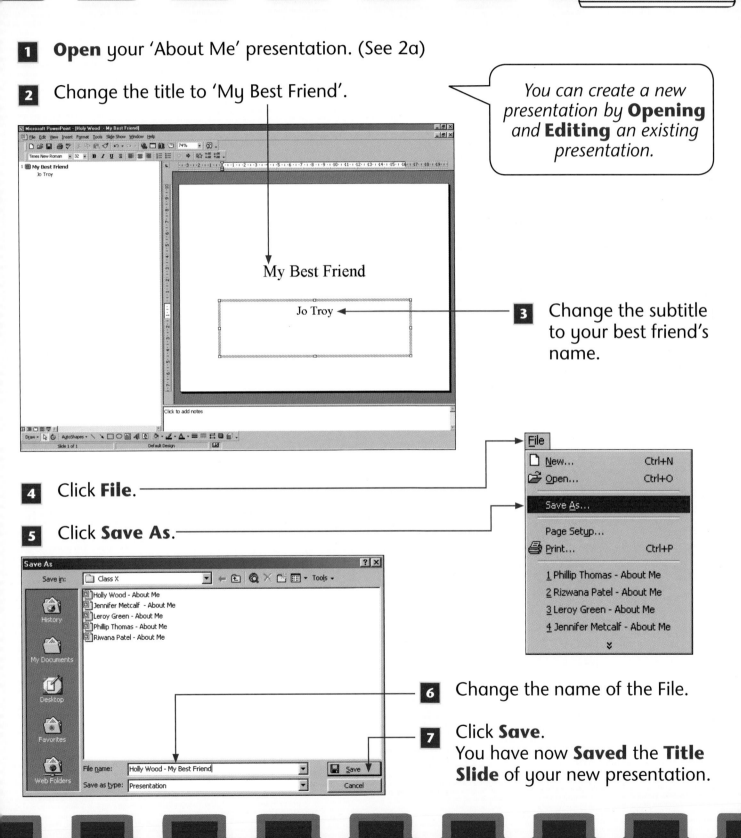

3 Change the subtitle to your best friend's name.

4 Click **File**.

5 Click **Save As**.

6 Change the name of the File.

7 Click **Save**.
You have now **Saved** the **Title Slide** of your new presentation.

Adding a New Slide

1 **Open** an existing presentation. (See 2a)

2 Click **Insert**.

3 Click **New Slide**.

4 Choose the **Layout** for your **New Slide** from the **AutoLayout** options.

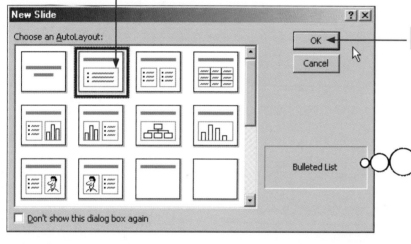

5 Click **OK**.
Your **New Slide** will **Open**.

> *Remember*
> *The name of the* **Slide** *you have selected appears here.*

6 Click the **Text Boxes** to add your text.

PowerPointWorks

My Appearance

SKILL: Adding a New Slide

The second slide of your presentation will describe how you look.

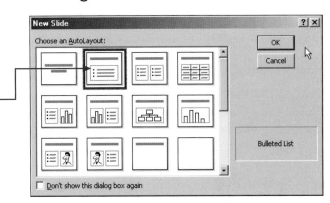

1 **Open** your 'About Me' presentation. (See 2a)

2 Select the **Bulleted List AutoLayout** for your **New Slide**. (See 3a)

3 Add the title 'My Appearance'.

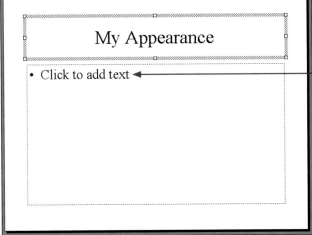

My Appearance

• Click to add text

4 Click next to the first **Bullet**.

5 Add your details.

> *When you are at the end of a sentence, press **Enter**. The next **Bullet** will appear automatically.*

6 **Save**.

> *The title and the details of the slides will appear in the **Outline Pane**.*

7 Use the **New Slide** icon to add a **New Slide** to your 'My Best Friend' presentation.

New Slide

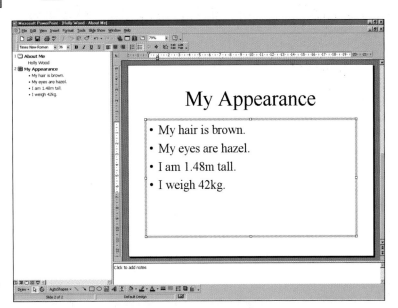

You can move from **Slide** to **Slide** in two different ways.

1 **Open** an existing presentation.

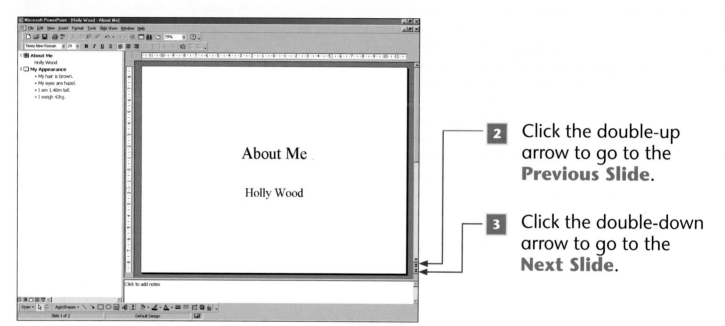

2 Click the double-up arrow to go to the **Previous Slide**.

3 Click the double-down arrow to go to the **Next Slide**.

OR

4 Click the number of the **Slide** you want to see.

Clicking the Slide number allows you to move to any Slide with one click. Clicking the double arrows allows you only to move up or down one Slide at a time.

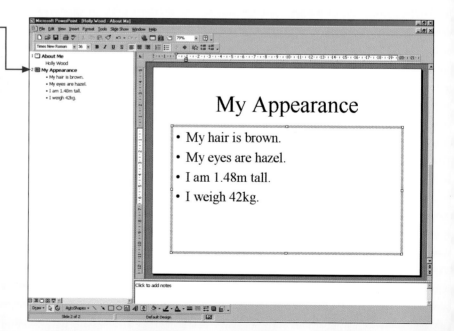

My Hobbies

1 **Open** your 'About Me' presentation.

2 Move to the **Slide** called 'My Appearance'. (See 4a)

3 Add your age to the list.

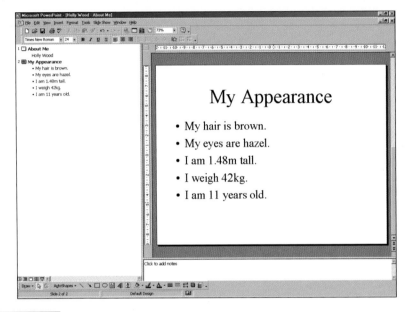

4 Insert a **New Slide**. Select the **Bulleted List AutoLayout**. (See 3a)

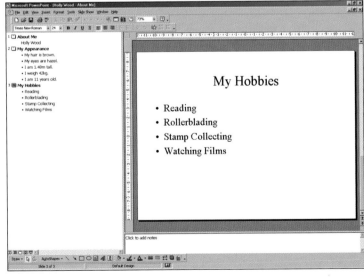

5 Add the title 'My Hobbies'.

6 List four of your hobbies.

7 **Save**.

8 Use the **New Slide** icon to add a similar **Slide** to your 'My Best Friend' presentation.

New Slide

Formatting Text

You can change the **Format** of the text in a **Text Box**.

1 **Open** an existing presentation.

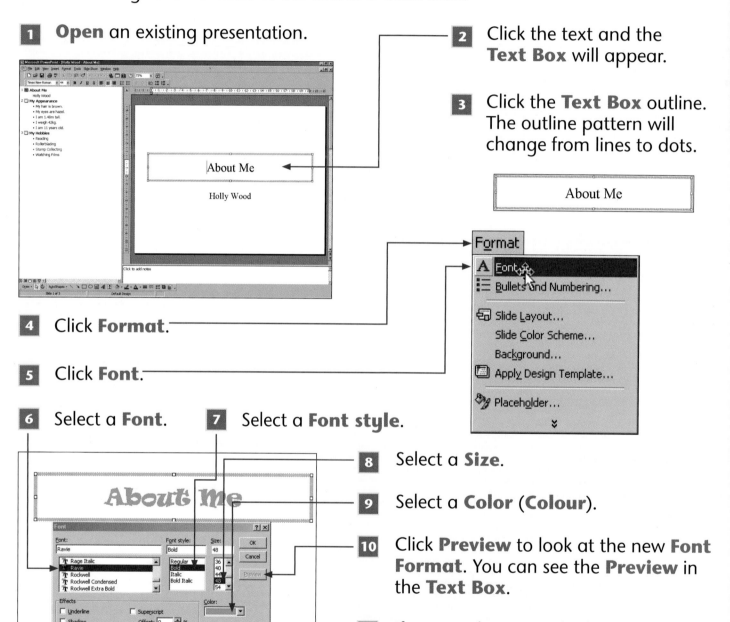

2 Click the text and the **Text Box** will appear.

3 Click the **Text Box** outline. The outline pattern will change from lines to dots.

4 Click **Format**.

5 Click **Font**.

6 Select a **Font**.

7 Select a **Font style**.

8 Select a **Size**.

9 Select a **Color** (**Colour**).

10 Click **Preview** to look at the new **Font Format**. You can see the **Preview** in the **Text Box**.

11 If you are happy with your choice, click **OK**.

*You can also change the **Format** of smaller amounts of text. Highlight the text you want to change. Go back to* **4** .

Change 'My Appearance'

SKILL: Formatting Text

APPLICATION

1 **Open** your 'About Me' presentation.

2 Move to the slide called 'My Appearance'. (See 4a)

3 Change the **Font**, **Font style**, **Font Size** and **Font Color** (**Colour**) of the title. (See 5a)

Remember Highlight only the text you want to change.

4 Change the **Font Format** of each point on your list.

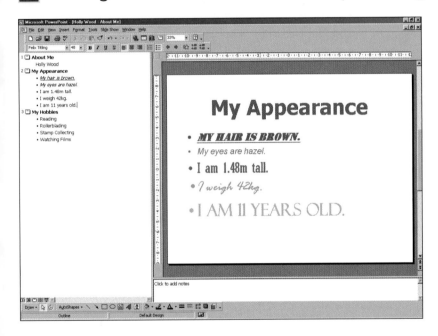

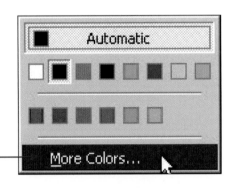

5 Click **More Colors** (**Colours**) for a wider choice of colours.

6 **Save**.

7 Change the **Font Format** in your 'My Best Friend' presentation.

*Try using **Effects** to create a different style.*

To use **Effects**:

- Click **Format**.
- Click **Font**.
- **Effects** options are in the lower half of the box.
- Tick the **Effect** option you want.

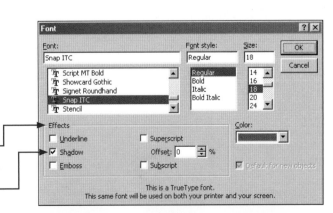

Aligning Text

You can change the **Alignment** of the text in your **Text Box**.

1 **Open** an existing presentation.

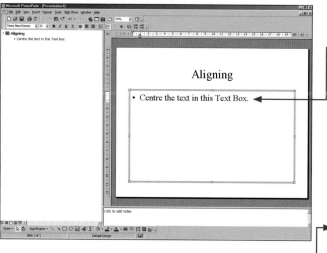

2 Click inside the **Text Box**.
The **Text Box** outline will appear.

3 Click the outline of the **Text Box** so that the line pattern turns to dots.

4 Click **Format**.

5 Click **Alignment**.

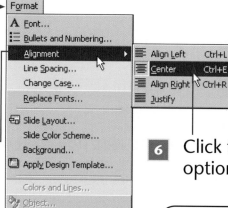

6 Click the **Alignment** option of your choice.

*You can also change the **Alignment** of individual lines by using the **Align** icons.*

- Click anywhere in the line you want to **Align**.

- Click the **Align** icon of your choice.

Align Left   Center (Centre)   Align Right

My Teacher

SKILL: Aligning Text

APPLICATION

1 Open a **New Blank Presentation**.

2 Create a **Title Slide**, 'My Teacher'. (See 1a)

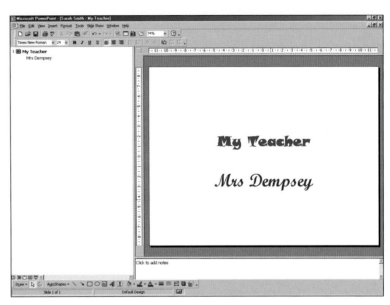

3 Type your teacher's name as the subtitle.

4 Change the **Font Format** and the **Font Colour** of the text. (See 5a)

5 Add a **New Slide** (**Bulleted List**).

6 Add the title 'What (teacher's name) Teaches'.

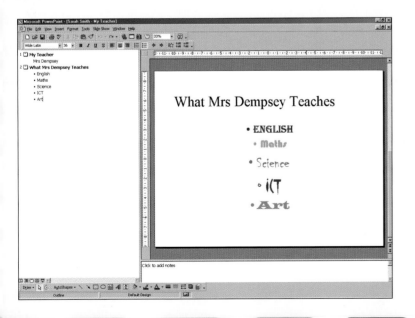

7 List the subjects your teacher teaches.

8 **Left Align** the title. (See 6a)

9 **Centre** the list.

10 Change the **Font Format** and **Font Colour** of each item on your list.

11 **Save**.

1 **Open** an existing presentation.

2 Select the **Text Box** containing the **Bulleted List**.

3 Click the outline of the **Text Box** so that the line pattern turns to dots.

My Appearance

- *MY HAIR IS BROWN.*
- *My eyes are hazel.*
- I am 1.48m tall.
- *I weigh 42kg.*
- I AM 11 YEARS OLD.

4 Click **Format**.

5 Click **Bullets and Numbering**.

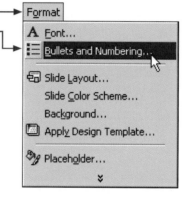

Format
A Font...
:≡ Bullets and Numbering...
🗐 Slide Layout...
 Slide Color Scheme...
 Background...
🖳 Apply Design Template...
🖎 Placeholder...
 ⌄

6 Click the **Numbered** tab.

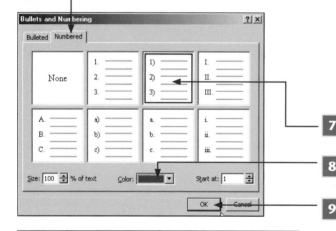

Bullets and Numbering

Bulleted | Numbered

None

1. 2. 3.

1) 2) 3)

I. II. III.

A. B. C.

a) b) c)

a. b. c.

i. ii. iii.

Size: 100 % of text   Color: Start at: 1

OK   Cancel

7 Click the **Numbering** style of your choice.

8 Select a **Color** (**Colour**) for the **Numbers**.

9 Click **OK**.

If you want to remove the **Bullets** *or* **Numbering**, *click* **None** *when you reach* **7** .

My Appearance

1) *MY HAIR IS BROWN.*
2) *My eyes are hazel.*
3) I am 1.48m tall.
4) *I weigh 42kg.*
5) I AM 11 YEARS OLD.

You can change **Bullets** to **Numbers** using these icons.

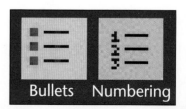

Bullets   Numbering

My Favourite Things

SKILL: Changing a Bulleted List to a Numbered List

APPLICATION

1 **Open** your 'About Me' presentation.

2 Move to the slide, 'My Hobbies'. (See 4a)

3 Insert a **New Slide** (**Bulleted List**). (See 3a)

4 Add the title 'My Favourite Things'.

5 Enter a list of your five favourite things.

6 Change the **Bulleted List** to a **Numbered List**. (See 7a)

7 Change the **Font** and the **Font Colour** of your list. (See 5a)

8 **Save**.

My Favourite Things

1. My mum
2. My stamp collection
3. My 'Harry Potter' book
4. My dog Benji
5. My new trainers.

9 **Open** your 'My Best Friend' presentation.

10 Create a **New Slide** listing your friend's favourite things from 1 to 5, using the **Numbering** icon.

Numbering

Formatting Bullets

You can change the style of an existing **Bulleted List** or add **Bullets** to text.

1 **Open** an existing presentation.

2 Select a **Text Box**.

3 Click the outline of the **Text Box** so that the line pattern turns to dots.

4 Click **Format**.

5 Click **Bullets and Numbering**.

6 Click the **Bulleted** tab.

7 Click **Picture**.

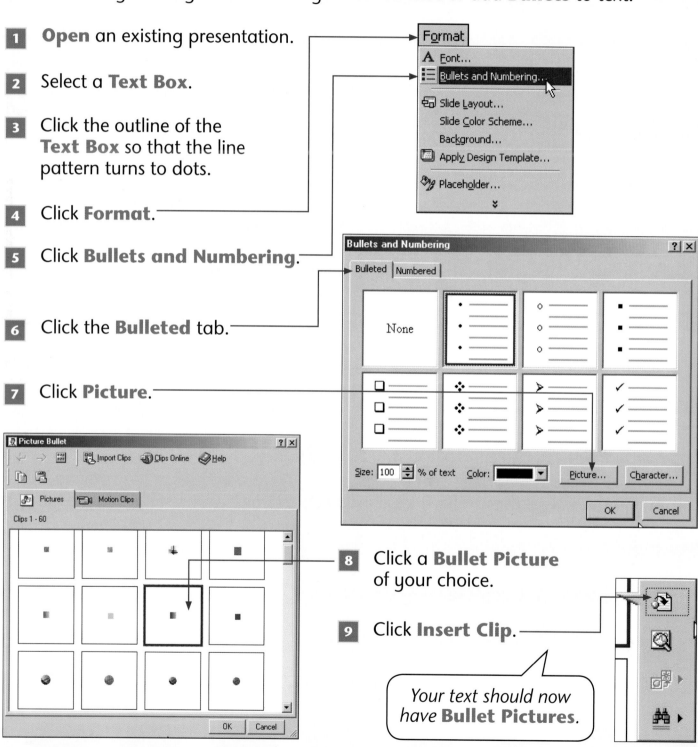

8 Click a **Bullet Picture** of your choice.

9 Click **Insert Clip**.

*Your text should now have **Bullet Pictures**.*

At the Farm

1 Open a **New Blank Presentation**.

2 Create a **Title Slide**, 'At the Farm'. (See 1a)

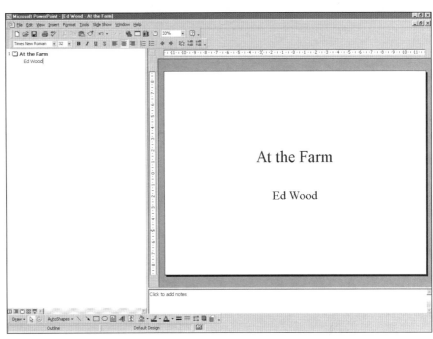

3 Type your name for the subtitle.

4 Insert a **New Slide (Bulleted List)**.

5 Add the title, 'Farm Animals'.

6 Select a new **Bullet Picture**. (See 8a)

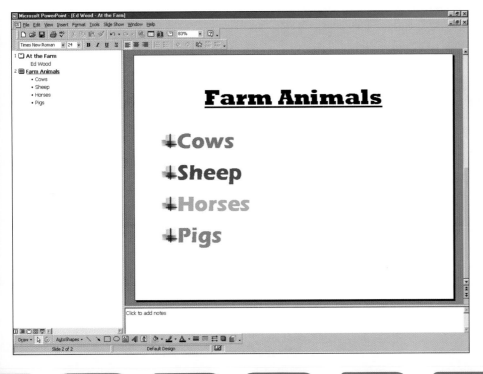

7 Type a list of four animals you would find on a farm.

8 Change the **Font** and the **Font Colour** of your list.

9 Save.

You can change the space between lines.

1 **Open** an existing presentation.

2 To create equal spaces between all the lines, click the line of the **Text Box** so the line pattern changes to dots.

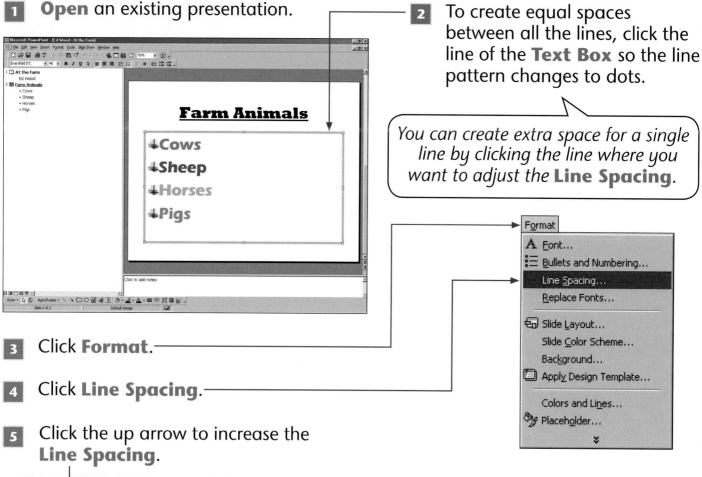

*You can create extra space for a single line by clicking the line where you want to adjust the **Line Spacing**.*

3 Click **Format**.

4 Click **Line Spacing**.

5 Click the up arrow to increase the **Line Spacing**.

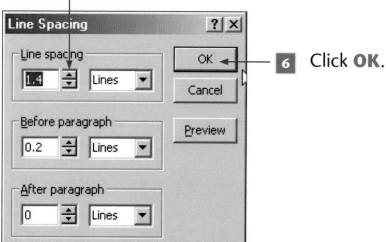

6 Click **OK**.

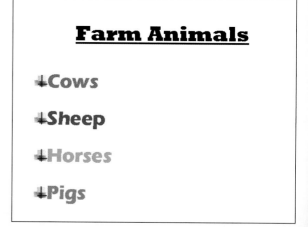

Farm Animals

SKILL: Changing Line Spacing

1 **Open** your 'At the Farm' presentation.

2 Move to the 'Farm Animals' slide.

3 Insert a **New Slide** (**Bulleted List**).

4 Select one of the animals on your list. This will be the title.

5 Type a list of four facts about this animal.

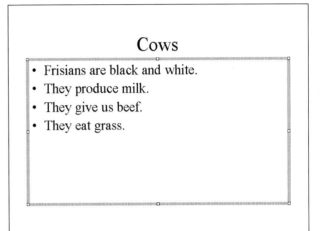

6 Use **Line Spacing** to change the spaces between the lines. (See 9a)

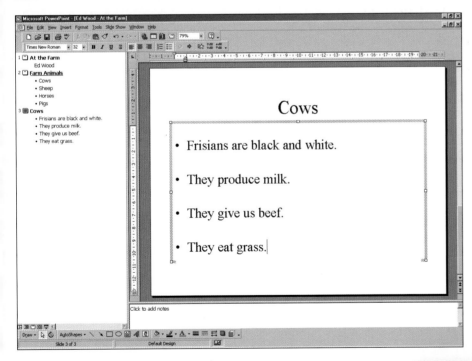

7 Change the **Line Spacing** again but use the icons.

8 **Save**.

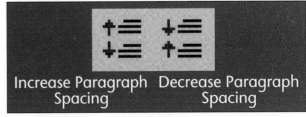

Increase Paragraph Spacing   Decrease Paragraph Spacing

Resizing and Moving a Text Box

1 Click the **Text Box**.

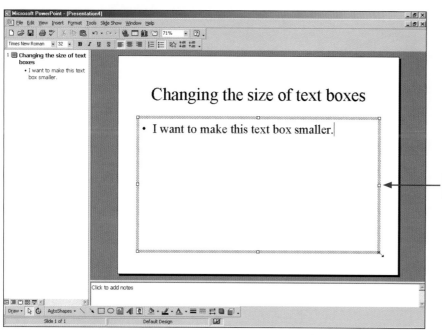

*You can increase and decrease the size of the **Text Box**. You can also reposition it.*

2 Place the cursor on one of the eight squares. It will change to a double-headed arrow ↕.

3 **Resize** the **Text Box**.

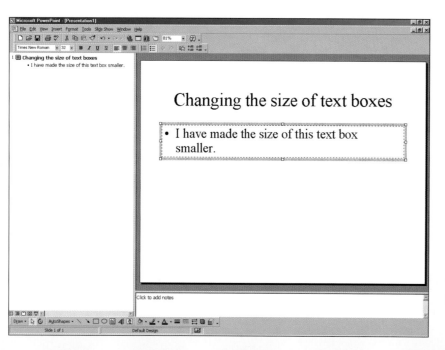

4 Let go of the mouse when the **Text Box** is the size you want.

5 If you want to reposition the **Text Box**, click and hold the outline of the **Text Box**. ✛ will appear.

6 Drag the **Text Box** to its new position.

1 Open a **New Blank Presentation**.

2 Create a **Title Slide**, 'School Dinners' with your name as the subtitle.

3 Insert a **New Slide** (**Bulleted List**).

> ## School Dinners
>
> Salim Patel

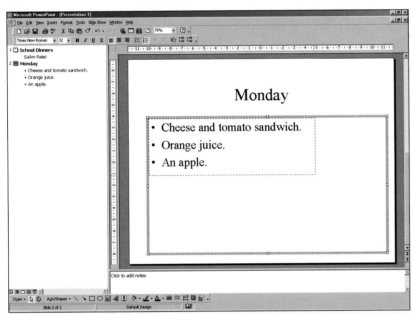

4 Type 'Monday' as the title.

5 List what you had for your school dinner on Monday.

6 **Resize** the **Text Box**. (See 10a)

7 Create a **New Slide** for every day of the school week.

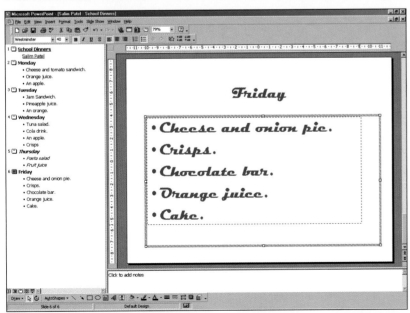

8 Change the **Font** and **Font Color** (**Colour**) of the text on each slide.

9 **Save**.

Adding a Text Box

1 **Open** an existing presentation.

2 Select a slide to which you want to add a **Text Box**.

3 Click **Insert**.

4 Click **Text Box**.

5 Click where you want to insert the **Text Box**. A small box will appear.

6 The cursor will flash. Type your text.

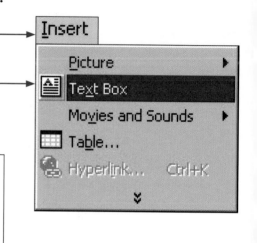

As you type the text box will increase in size.

7 Click outside the **Text Box** when you have finished.

Deleting a Text Box

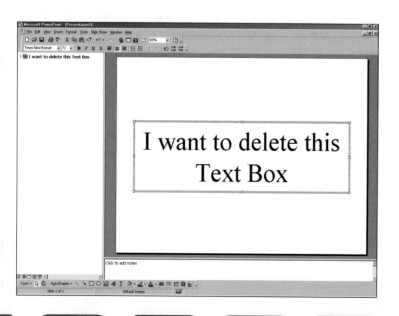

8 Click the line of the **Text Box** so that the line pattern turns to dots.

9 Press **Delete**.

Where I Live

APPLICATION

SKILL: Adding and Deleting a Text Box

1 Open a **New Blank Presentation**.

2 Create a **Title Slide**.

3 Add the title, 'Where I Live'.

4 **Delete** the subtitle **Text Box**. (See 11a)

5 Create a **New Slide** (**Blank Slide**).

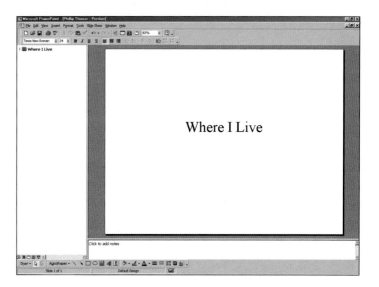

6 **Insert** a **Text Box** and add the name of the place where you live.

7 **Insert** a second **Text Box** and add a list of four facts about the place where you live.

> You might add information about:
> ● Location
> ● Population
> ● Places of interest
> ● Cinemas or theatres.

8 Change the **Font**, **Font Size** and **Font Colour** of the text on your slide.

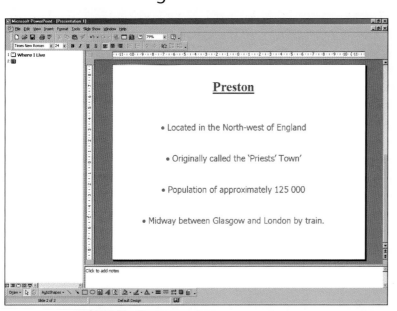

9 **Centre** the text. (See 6a)

> **Remember**
> You need to highlight the text before you **Align** it.

10 Change the **Line Spacing** to fill the slide. (See 9a)

11 **Save**.

Formatting a Text Box

Adding a Fill Color (Colour) to a Text Box

1 Click the **Text Box**.

2 Click the arrow next to the **Fill Color** (**Colour**) icon.

3 Click a **Color** (**Colour**).

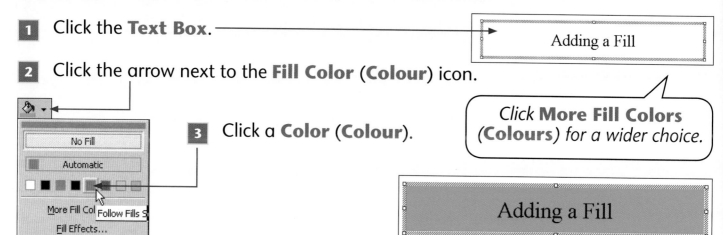

No Fill
Automatic
More Fill Col... Follow Fills S...
Fill Effects...

> *Click **More Fill Colors** (**Colours**) for a wider choice.*

Adding a Fill

Adding a Fill

Adding a Border to a Text Box

4 Click the **Text Box**.

5 Click the **Line Style** icon.

6 Click a **Line Style**.

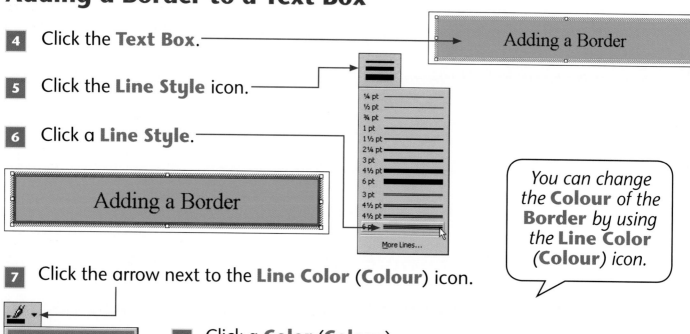

¼ pt
½ pt
¾ pt
1 pt
1½ pt
2¼ pt
3 pt
4½ pt
6 pt
3 pt
4½ pt
4½ pt
6 pt
More Lines...

Adding a Border

Adding a Border

> *You can change the **Colour** of the **Border** by using the **Line Color** (**Colour**) icon.*

7 Click the arrow next to the **Line Color** (**Colour**) icon.

8 Click a **Color** (**Colour**).

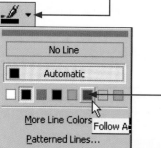

No Line
Automatic
More Line Colors Follow A...
Patterned Lines...

Adding a Border

A Colourful Place to Live

1 **Open** your 'Where I Live' presentation.

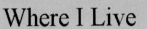

2 Select the **Title Slide** and add a background colour and **Border**. Use the **Fill Color, Line Style** and **Line Color** icons. (See 12a)

 Fill Color (Colour)  Line Style  Line Color (Colour)

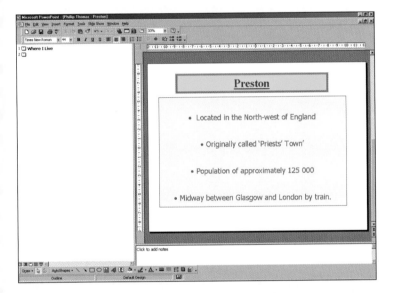

3 Move to the next slide and add a **Border** and **Fill Colours** to the **Text Boxes**.

4 Create a **New Slide (Bulleted List)**.

5 Add the title, 'Why I like (your town)'.

6 Type two reasons why you like living there.

7 **Resize** the **Text Box**. (See 10a)

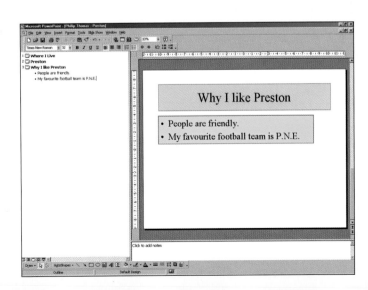

8 Add a **Fill Colour** and a **Border** to the title's **Text Box** and the **Text Box** containing your reasons.

9 **Save**.

Changing the Slide Background Colour

SKILL

You can change the **Background Colour** of one slide or of all the slides in your presentation.

1 **Open** an existing presentation.

2 Click **Format**.————————

3 Click **Background**.————————

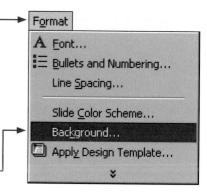

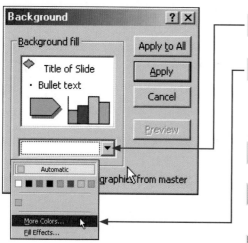

4 Click the down arrow.

5 Click **More Colors** (**Colours**).

6 Click a colour.————

7 Click **OK**.————

8 Click **Apply** to change the **Background Colour** of one slide.

Changing the Background

I have changed the background colour of this slide.

> *If you want the same **Background Colour** on all the slides, click **Apply to All**.*

1 Open a **New Blank Presentation**.

2 Create a **Title Slide**, 'Colours of the Rainbow'.

3 Insert a **New Slide** (**Title Only**).

Colours of the Rainbow

4 Type the first colour of the rainbow in the **Text Box**.

5 Change the **Background Colour** to match. (See 13a)

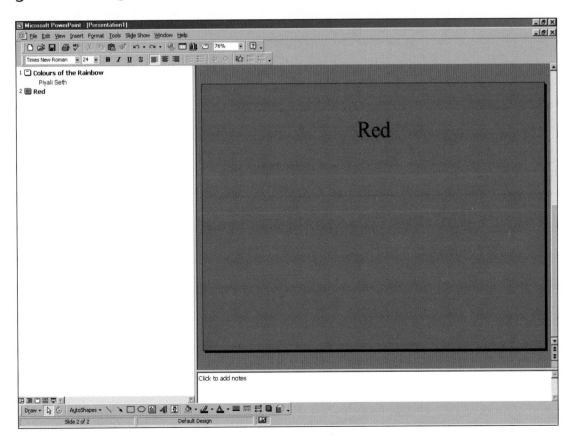

6 Insert a **New Slide** for each of the other six colours of the rainbow and change the **Background Colours** to match.

7 **Save**.

14a

SKILL

1 **Open** an existing presentation.

2 Click **Insert**.

3 Move to **Picture**.

4 Click **ClipArt**.

5 Click the **Pictures** tab.

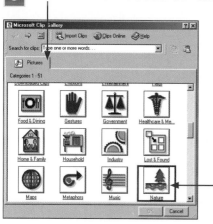

6 Click the category of **ClipArt** that you want.

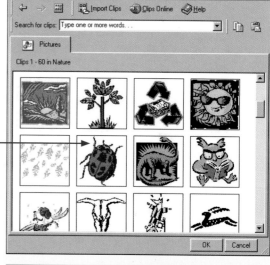

7 Click the image of your choice.

8 Click the **Insert Clip** icon.

9 Click **Close**. ✕

Your **ClipArt** will be inserted.

Ladybird

My Favourite Animal

SKILL: Adding ClipArt

1 **Open** your 'About Me' presentation.

2 Create a **New Slide** (**Text & ClipArt**).

3 Add the title 'My Favourite Animal'.

4 In the **Text Box**, type a reason why you like that animal.

5 **Insert ClipArt** of your animal. (See 14a)

*There are two slides in the **AutoLayout** options that are designed so that you can **Insert ClipArt**.*

Text & ClipArt   ClipArt & Text

*If you choose to use an **AutoLayout**:*
- *Insert one of the two slide options.*
- *Double-click the **ClipArt** placeholder.*
- *Follow instructions* **5** *to* **9** *on 14a.*
- *Add a title and text.*

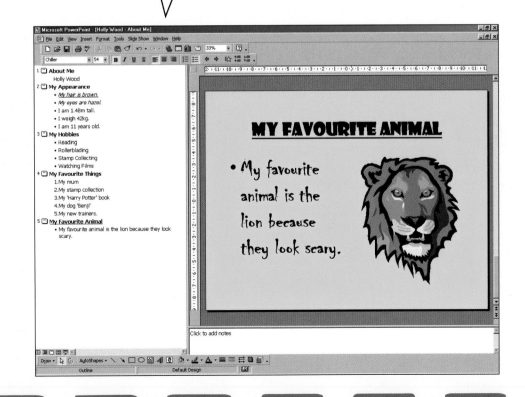

SKILL 15a

You can change the size, position and colours of **ClipArt**.

Resizing ClipArt

Resizing ClipArt

1 Open a **New Blank Presentation** and insert a **Slide** (**Title Only**).

2 Add a title and insert a **ClipArt** image. (See 14a)

3 To reduce or enlarge the **ClipArt**, drag any small box.

Moving ClipArt

4 Click the **ClipArt** until you see ⬍. **5** Move the **ClipArt**.

Recolouring ClipArt

6 Click the **ClipArt**.

7 Click the **Recolor** (**Recolour**) **Picture** icon on the **Picture** toolbar.

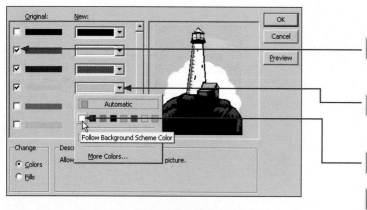

8 Click a tick next to the colours you want to change.

9 Click the down arrow next to the colour you want to change.

10 Select a new colour.

11 Click **OK**.

Restoring ClipArt

12 To **Restore** the **ClipArt** to the original colours, click the **Reset Picture** icon.

My Day

1 Open a **New Blank Presentation**.

2 Create a **Title Slide**, 'My Day'.

3 Type your name as the subtitle.

4 Insert a **New Slide** (**Text & ClipArt**).

5 Add the title 'Morning'.

6 Add a sentence about your morning routine.

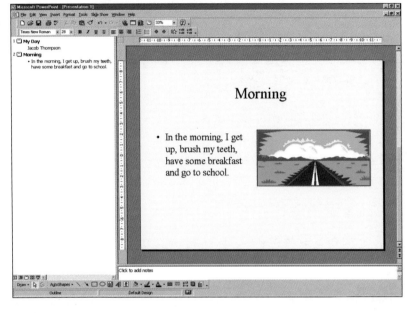

7 Insert a **ClipArt** picture of a daytime scene. (See 14a)

8 **Resize** the picture. (See 15a)

9 Using the **Recolor** (**Recolour**) icon, change the colours to give the impression of daybreak.

10 Change the background colour of the slide. (See 13a)

11 Insert another **Slide** (**ClipArt & Text**) called 'Evening'.

12 Insert the picture of a daytime scene and **Recolour** the picture to give the impression of evening.

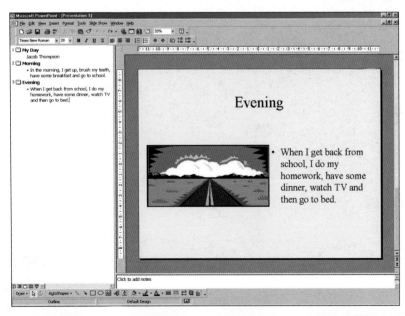

13 **Save**.

16a Adding AutoShapes with Text

SKILL

You can use **AutoShapes** to improve the appearance of your presentation.

1 Open a **New Blank Presentation**.

2 Create a **New Slide** (**Blank**).

*In PowerPoint, you can type text inside all **AutoShapes**.*

3 Click **Insert**.

4 Click **Picture**.

5 Click **AutoShapes**.

Insert
- New Slide... Ctrl+M
- Picture ▸
  - Clip Art...
  - From File...
  - AutoShapes
  - Organization Chart
  - WordArt...
- Text Box
- Movies and Sounds ▸
- Table...
- Object...
- Hyperlink... Ctrl+K

6 Click an **AutoShape** category.

AutoShapes

7 Click an **AutoShape**.

Heart

8 Click a small box and drag the mouse until the **AutoShape** is the size you want.

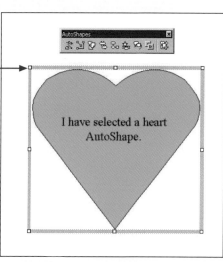

I have selected a heart AutoShape.

9 Type your text.

*When you draw an **AutoShape**, the **Fill Color** (**Colour**) appears automatically.*

PowerPointWorks

Keeping Healthy

SKILL: Adding AutoShapes with Text

16b

Use **AutoShapes** to enhance a presentation.

1 Open a **New Blank Presentation**.

2 Create the first **Slide** (**Blank**) 'Keeping Healthy', using an **AutoShape**. (See 16a)

> *The text you type in 'objects', such as **Text Boxes** and **AutoShapes**, does not appear in the **Outline Pane**.*

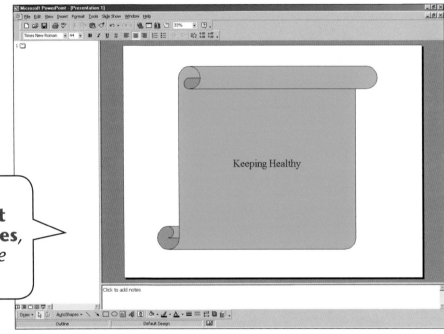

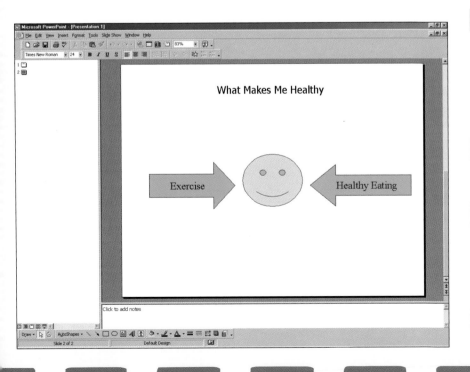

3 **Insert** a **New Slide** (**Blank**). In a **Text Box**, add the title, 'What Makes Me Healthy'. (See 11a)

4 Use an **AutoShape** to represent you.

5 Create a diagram using **AutoShapes** with text to show what makes you healthy.

6 **Save**.

PowerPointWorks

17a

SKILL

1 **Open** an existing presentation that contains an **AutoShape** with text.

2 Click the **AutoShape**.

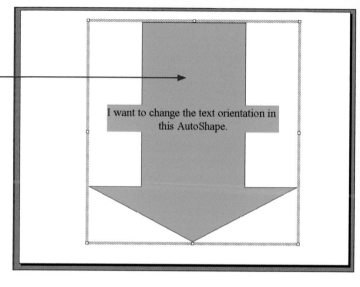

I want to change the text orientation in this AutoShape.

3 Click **Format**.

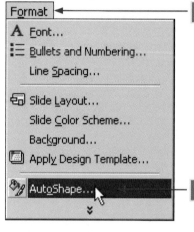

Format
A Font...
≡ Bullets and Numbering...
Line Spacing...
Slide Layout...
Slide Color Scheme...
Background...
Apply Design Template...
AutoShape...

4 Click **AutoShape**.

5 Click the **Text Box** tab.

6 Click **Rotate text within AutoShape by 90°**.

7 Click **OK**.

Format AutoShape

Colors and Lines | Size | Position | Picture | Text Box | Web

Text anchor point: Middle

Internal margin
Left: 0.25 cm   Top: 0.13 cm
Right: 0.25 cm   Bottom: 0.13 cm

☐ Word wrap text in AutoShape
☐ Resize AutoShape to fit text
☑ Rotate text within AutoShape by 90°

OK   Cancel   Preview

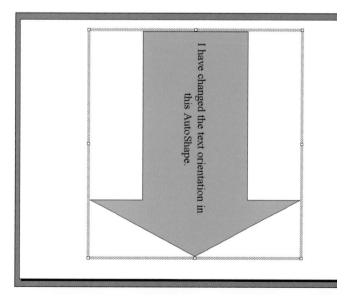

I have changed the text orientation in this AutoShape.

Choose **Text Box** or **Table** on the **Format Menu** to change the **Text Orientation** in the same way as with **AutoShapes**.

Healthy Foods

SKILL: Changing Text Orientation

APPLICATION

1 **Open** your 'Keeping Healthy' presentation.

2 Select the 'What Makes Me Healthy' slide.

3 Add more **AutoShapes**. (See 16a)

4 Change the **Text Orientation**. (See 17a)

5 Insert a **New Slide** (**Blank**) 'Healthy Eating' and add a **Smiley Face AutoShape**.

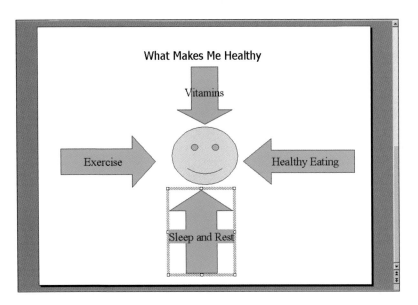

6 Use **Block Arrows** to show the main elements of a healthy, balanced diet.
- Bread, Cereals and Potatoes – Carbohydrates and Fibre
- Dairy Produce – Calcium, Protein, Fats and Sugars
- Fatty and Sugary Foods
- Fruit and Vegetables – Vitamins and Minerals
- Meat, Fish and Beans – Protein.

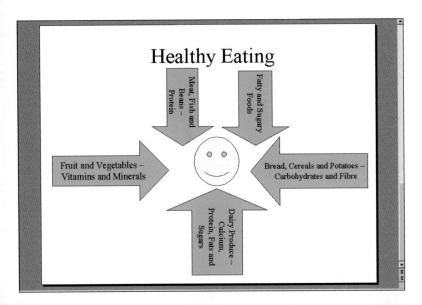

7 You might need to change the **Font Size** of the text.

8 Change the **Text Orientation**.

9 **Save**.

Creating Shadows

You can improve the appearance of your slides by adding **Shadows**.

Adding a Shadow to an AutoShape

1 Click to select the **AutoShape**.

2 Click the **Shadow** icon.

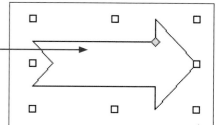

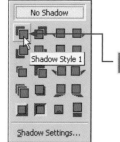

3 Click a **Shadow Style**.

*The **Shadow** will be added.*

Changing the Colour of the Shadow

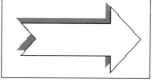

4 Click the **AutoShape** to which you have added a **Shadow**.

5 Click **Shadow Settings**.

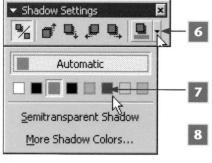

6 Click the **Shadow Color** (**Colour**) arrow.

7 Select a new colour.

8 Click ☒ to **Close** the toolbar.

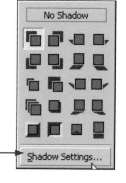

Adding Shadows to Text

9 Click the **Text Box**.

I want to add a shadow to this text.

10 Go back to **2** and follow the instructions to **3**.

I have added a shadow to this text.

Shapes

SKILL: Creating Shadows

18b

APPLICATION

1 Open a **New Blank Presentation**.

2 Create a **Title Slide**, 'Shapes'.

3 Add your name to the **Title Slide**.

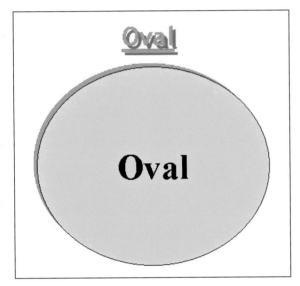

Shapes

Phillip Thomas

4 Insert a **New Slide** (**Title Only**) with the title, 'Oval'.

5 Add a **Shadow** to the title.

6 Insert an **Oval AutoShape**, label it and add a **Shadow** to it. (See 16a and 18a)

7 Change the colour of the **Shadow**.

8 Insert a **New Slide** for each of the following shapes:
- Right-angled Triangle
- Rectangle
- Hexagon
- Octagon.

Add **Shadows** to each title and shape.

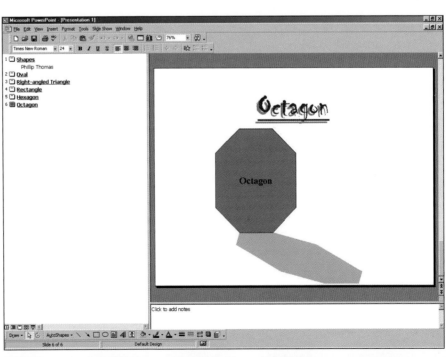

Adding a 3-D Style

1 Open a **New Blank Presentation**.

2 Insert an **AutoShape** on a **New Slide** (**Blank**).

3 Click the **AutoShape** to select it.

4 Click the **3-D** icon.

5 Click a **3-D Style**.

Tilting the 3-D AutoShape

6 Click the **AutoShape** to select it.

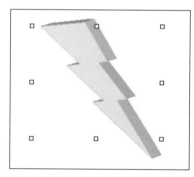

7 Click the **3-D** icon and click **3-D Settings**.

8 Choose a **Tilt** direction.

9 Click ☒ to **Close** the toolbar.

Set the 3-D Depth Size

10 Go to **6** and follow the instructions to **7**.

11 Click the **Depth** icon.

12 Select a **Depth Size**.

13 Click ☒ to **Close** the toolbar.

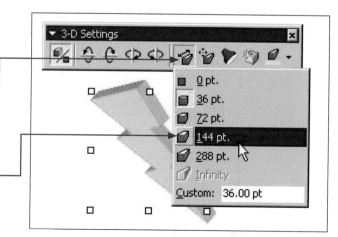

3-D Shapes

SKILL: Creating 3-D Styles

1 **Open** your 'Shapes' presentation.

2 Insert a **New Slide (Title Only)** 'Cylinder'.

3 Insert an **Oval AutoShape**.

4 Change the oval to a cylinder using the **3-D** icon. (See 19a)

5 Change the **Colour** and **Tilt** of the **3-D AutoShape**.

6 Increase the **Depth**.

7 Label the **3-D AutoShape** as a 'Cylinder'.

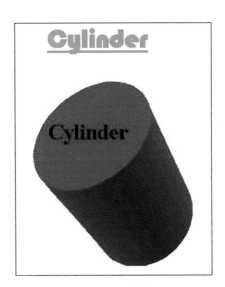

8 Use 2-D **AutoShapes** to create the following **3-D AutoShapes**:

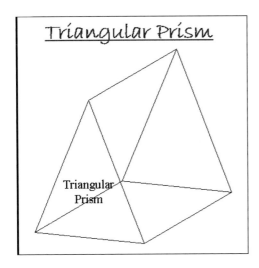

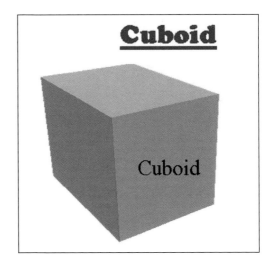

9 Now create **New Slides** for more 3-D shapes.

10 **Save**.

Adding a Table

You can use **Tables** to display information in your presentation.

> *You can insert a **Table** in two ways.*

Insert a Table Slide

1 Insert a **New Slide** in an existing presentation.

2 Select the **Table AutoLayout**.

Table

3 Double-click the **Text Box**.

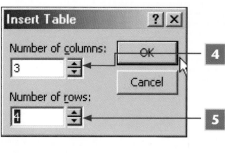

4 Select the **Number of columns**.

5 Select the **Number of rows**.

6 Click **OK**.

Table AutoLayout

Double click to add table

Insert a Table on a Blank Slide

7 Click **Insert**.

8 Click **Table**.

9 Go to **4** and follow the instructions to **6** .

Insert
- New Slide...   Ctrl+M
- Picture ▶
- Te**x**t Box
- Mo**v**ies and Sounds ▶
- Table...
- Object...
- Hyperlink...   Ctrl+K

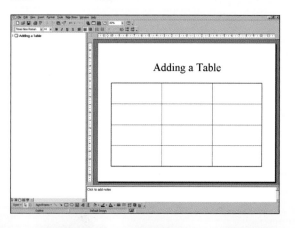

Adding a Table

> *You can use this method if you want to add a **Table** to a slide that has other information on it, for example, text or **ClipArt**.*

Shape Table

SKILL: Adding a Table

1 **Open** your 'Shapes' presentation.

2 Create a **New Slide (Table Slide)**. (See 20a)

3 **Insert** a **Table** with **2 Columns** and **6 Rows**.

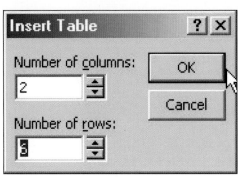

4 Label the **Table** as shown on the slide below and fill in the answers. Change the **Font, Font colour, Font Size** and **Background Colour** of the slide. (See 13a)

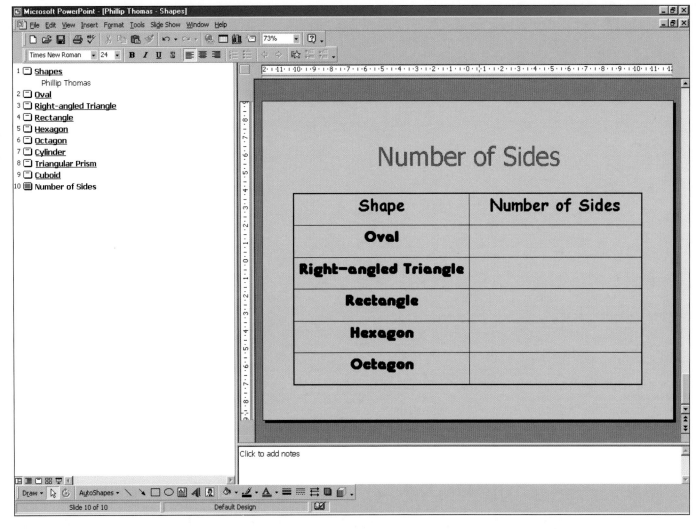

5 **Save**.

21a SKILL

Changing Column Width and Row Height

1 **Open** an existing presentation that contains a **Table**.

2 Move the cursor onto the line of the **Column** or **Row** that you want to change until it changes to: ⇕ .

3 Drag the line to the **Width** or **Depth** that you want.

Inserting and Deleting Rows

4 To **Delete** a **Row**, click anywhere in the **Row** you want to **Delete**.

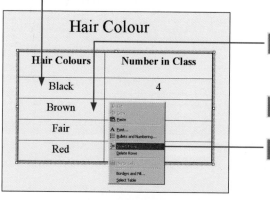

5 To **Insert** a **Row**, click anywhere in the **Row** below where you want the **Row** to appear.

6 Click the **Right Mouse Button**.

7 Click either **Insert Rows** or **Delete Rows**.

Formatting the Table

8 Click the **Table**.

9 Click **Format**.

*You will change the colour only of the **Cell** containing the cursor, unless you highlight all the **Cells** you wish to change.*

10 Click **Table**.

11 Click the **Fill** tab.

12 Click a colour.

13 Click **OK**.

SKILL: Editing a Table

21b

APPLICATION

1 **Open** your 'Shapes' presentation.

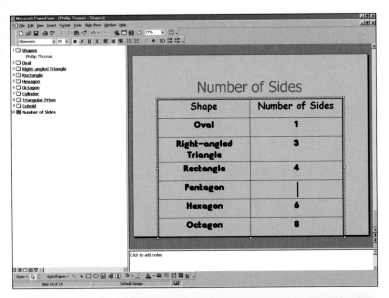

2 Select the **Table**.

3 **Insert** a **Row** between 'Rectangle' and 'Hexagon'. (See 21a)

4 Type 'Pentagon' and the number of sides it has.

5 **Resize** the **Table**.

> To **Resize** a **Table**, use the same method that you would use to **Resize** a **Text Box** or **ClipArt**. (See 10a)

6 Change the **Fill Colours** of the **Table**.

7 Insert a **New Slide** after the 'Rectangle' **Slide** and add an **AutoShape** of a regular pentagon.

8 Add a **Shadow** to your shape. (See 18a)

9 **Save**.

Inserting Movies

There are two different ways to add a **Movie** to your slide.

1 **Insert** a **New Slide** (**Text & Media Clip** or **Media Clip & Text**).

2 Double-click the **Box** to add a **Media Clip**.

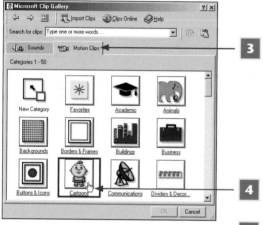

3 Click the **Motion Clips** tab.

4 Select a **Category**.

5 Select a **Clip**.

6 Click the **Insert Clip** icon.

7 Click **Close**.

OR

8 Click **Insert**.

9 Click **Movies and Sounds**.

10 Click **Movie from Gallery**.

11 Go back to **4** and follow the instructions to **7**.

> To **Preview** the Movie, click the **Play Clip** icon.

What I Like To Do

SKILL: Inserting Movies

APPLICATION

1 **Open** your 'About Me' presentation.

2 Insert a **New Slide** (**Text & Media Clip** or **Media Clip & Text**).

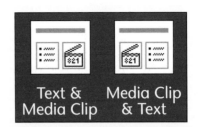

Text & Media Clip   Media Clip & Text

3 Add the title, 'What I Like To Do'.

4 Add a background colour to the slide.

5 **Insert** a **Movie** that best describes what you like to do. (See 22a)

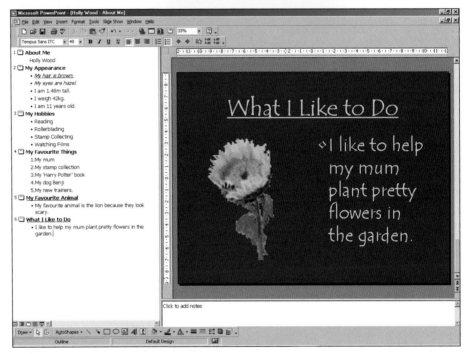

6 Type a sentence in the **Text Box** about the **Movie**.

7 Change the **Font**, **Font style** and **Font Color** (**Colour**) of the text.

8 **Save**.

9 **Open** your 'My Best Friend' presentation and repeat the process to create a slide that describes what your best friend likes to do.

Inserting Movies from CD

1 Create a **New Blank Presentation**.

2 Click **Insert**.

3 Click **Movies and Sounds**.

4 Click **Movie from File**.

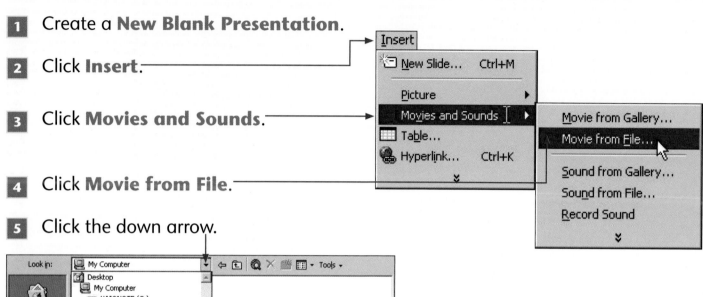

5 Click the down arrow.

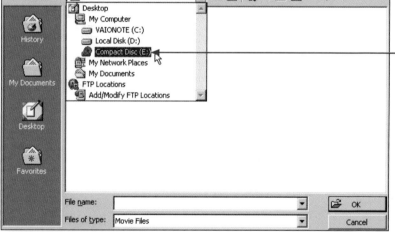

6 Click the **CD** drive.

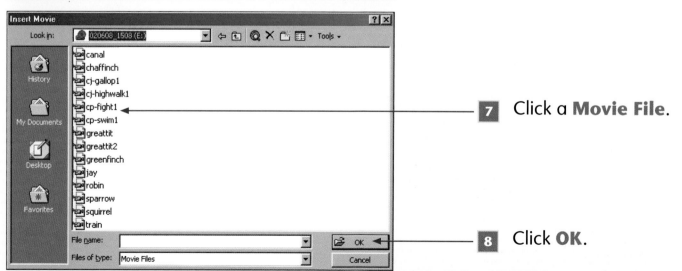

7 Click a **Movie File**.

8 Click **OK**.

PowerPointWorks

A Train Journey

SKILL: Inserting Movies from CD

APPLICATION

23b

1 Create a **New Blank Presentation**.

2 Insert a **Title Slide**, 'A Train Journey'.

3 Insert a **New Slide**. (**Text & Media Clip** or **Media Clip & Text**)

4 Add the title 'Where I Went'.

5 Add a background colour to the slide.

A Train Journey
Lloyd Gemson

6 Insert a **Movie** from a CD that shows a train. (See 23a)

7 Add a couple of sentences in the **Text Box** about where you went.

8 Change the **Font**, **Font style** and **Font Colour** of the text.

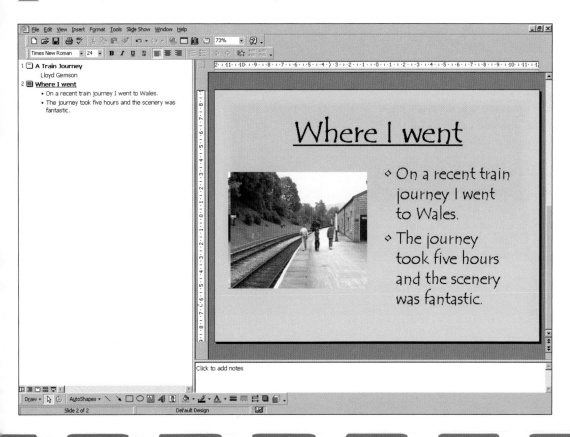

9 Save.

There are two different ways to add **Sounds** to your slide.

1 Insert a **New Slide** (**Text & Media Clip** or **Media Clip & Text**).

2 Double-click the **Box** to add a **Media Clip**.

3 Click the **Sounds** tab.

> To Preview *the Sound,*
> *click the* **Play Clip** *icon.*
>
>

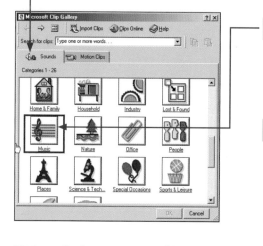

4 Select **Music** or **Entertainment** category.

5 Click a **Sound**.

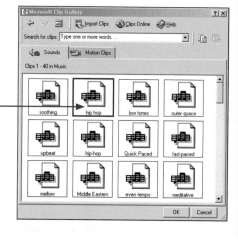

6 Click **Insert Clip**.

7 Click **Yes**, if you want the **Sound** to play automatically in your **Slide Show**, or **No**, if you want the **Sound** to play when you click it.

Microsoft PowerPoint

? Do you want your sound to play automatically in the slide show? If not, it will play when you click it.

Yes   No

OR

8 Click **Insert**.

9 Click **Movies and Sounds**.

10 Click **Sound from Gallery**.

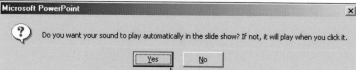

Insert
New Slide...   Ctrl+M
Picture   ▶
Movies and Sounds   ▶   Movie from Gallery...
Table...   Movie from File...
Hyperlink...   Ctrl+K   Sound from Gallery...
    Sound from File...

11 Go to **5** and follow the instructions to **7**.

My Favourite Music

SKILL: Inserting Sound

1 **Open** your 'About Me' presentation.

2 Insert a **New Slide** (**Media Clip & Text**).

3 Add the title, 'My Favourite Music'.

4 Add a background colour to the slide.

5 **Insert** a **Sound** that is similar to the type of music that you like. (See 24a)

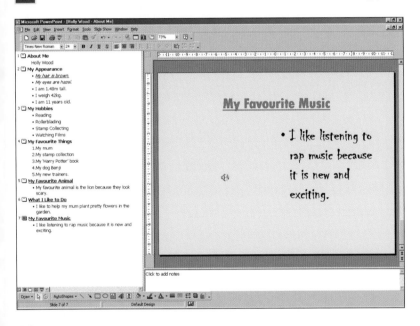

6 Add a sentence about the type of music to which you like to listen.

7 Change the **Font**, **Font style** and **Font Colour** of the text.

8 **Save**.

9 **Open** your 'My Best Friend' presentation and repeat the process to create a slide that includes your best friend's favourite music.

*If you have not set the **Sound** to play automatically, click the speaker when you reach the slide in the **Slide Show**.*

25a SKILL

Adding Tracks from a CD

1 Create a **New Slide**.

2 Place your music CD in the **CD drive**.

3 Click **Insert**.

4 Click **Movies and Sounds**.

5 Click **Play CD Audio Track**.

Insert menu:
- ⊡ New Slide... Ctrl+M
- Picture ▶
- Movies and Sounds ▶
  - Movie from Gallery...
  - Movie from File...
  - Sound from Gallery...
  - Sound from File...
  - Play CD Audio Track...
  - Record Sound
- ⊞ Table...
- 🌐 Hyperlink... Ctrl+K
- ⌄

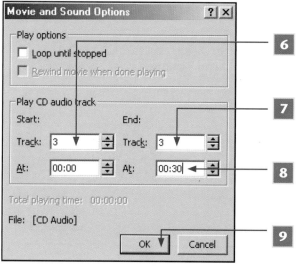

Movie and Sound Options

Play options
- ☐ Loop until stopped
- ☐ Rewind movie when done playing

Play CD audio track
Start: End:
Track: 3   Track: 3
At: 00:00   At: 00:30

Total playing time: 00:00:00
File: [CD Audio]

OK   Cancel

6 Enter the **Track Number** of the **Track** that you want to play.

7 Enter the **Track Number** of the **Track** at which you want to stop.

8 Enter the duration of time that you want to play the **Track**.

9 Click **OK**.

10 Click **Yes**, if you want the **CD Track** to play automatically in your **Slide Show**, or **No**, if you want the **Track** to play when you click the **CD Track** icon.

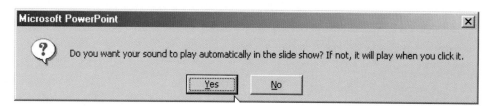

Microsoft PowerPoint

? Do you want your sound to play automatically in the slide show? If not, it will play when you click it.

Yes   No

*A **CD Track** icon will now appear on your slide. You can test play the track by double-clicking the **CD Track** icon.*

CD Track

My Favourite Pop Singer

SKILL: Adding Tracks from a CD

1 Open a **New Blank Presentation**.

2 Create a **Title Slide** called 'My Favourite Pop Singer'.

3 Create a presentation about your favourite pop singer.

4 On three slides include:
- Why you like them
- What type of music they sing
- The albums they have made.

5 Add a background colour to each slide.

6 Add a CD track from one of their albums to each of the slides. (See 25a)

7 Change the **Font**, **Font style** and **Font Colour** of the text.

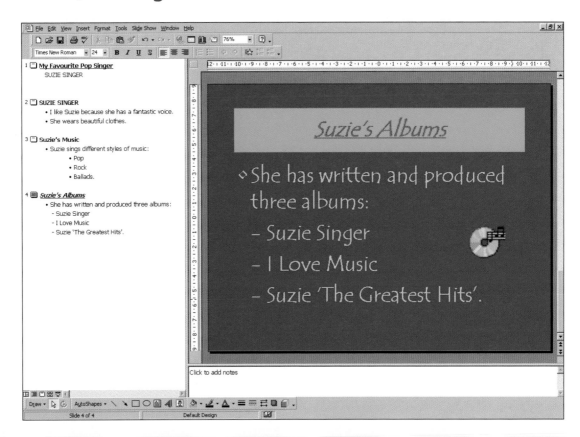

8 Save.

The slide numbers appear in the **Outline Pane**. You can also number your slides.

1 **Open** an existing presentation.

2 Move your cursor in the **Text Box** to where you want to insert your **Slide Number**.

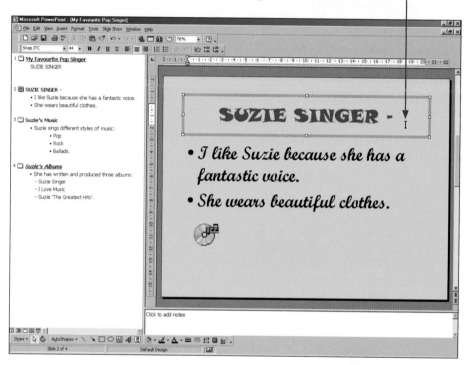

3 Click **Insert**.

4 Click **Slide Number**.
Your **Slide Number** will now be shown.

A Member of My Family

1 **Open** your 'About Me' presentation.

2 Create a **New Slide (Bulleted List)** 'A Member of My Family'.

3 Add a few sentences about a member of your family.

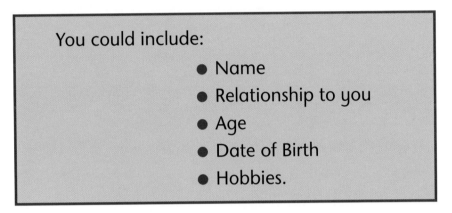

You could include:
- Name
- Relationship to you
- Age
- Date of Birth
- Hobbies.

4 Click the title **Text Box** and insert the **Slide Number**. (See 26a)

5 Add the **Slide Number** to each of the slides in your presentation.

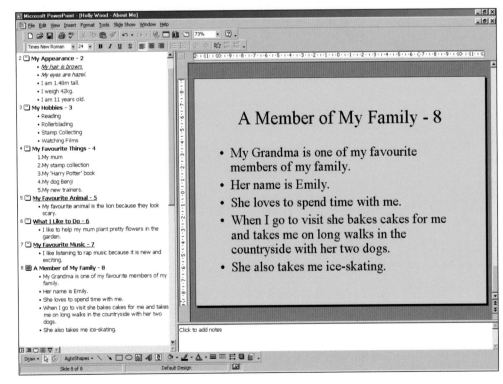

6 **Save**.

7 Add **Slide Numbers** to your 'My Best Friend' presentation.

Creating a Colour Scheme

You can change the colour of different parts of your slide.

1 Click **Format**.

2 Click **Slide Color (Colour) Scheme**.

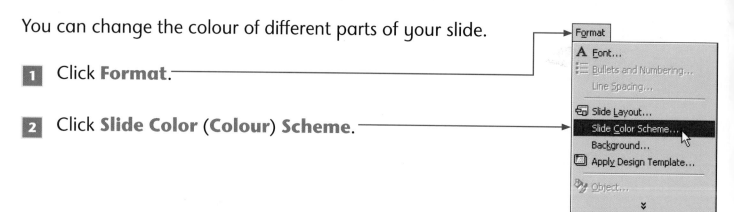

3 Click the **Custom** tab.

4 Click the area that you want to change.

5 Click **Change Color (Colour)**.

6 Click a colour.

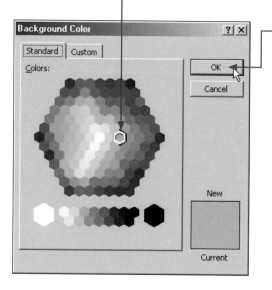

7 Click **OK**.

8 Repeat the process to change the colours of the different parts of the slide.

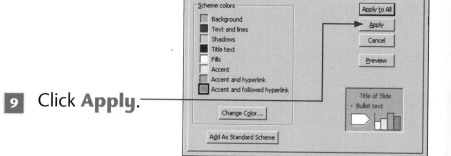

9 Click **Apply**.

PowerPointWorks

Rooms in My House

SKILL: Creating a Colour Scheme

APPLICATION

1 Open a **New Blank Presentation**.

2 Create a **Slide (Title Only)** 'Rooms In My House'.

3 Create a **Slide (Bulleted List)** for each of the rooms in your house.

4 Add a couple of sentences about each room.

5 Change the **Colour Scheme** of each of the slides to match the colour scheme of the room. (See 27a)

My Bedroom - 2

• My bedroom is at the front of the house.
• It overlooks the park.

6 Add **Slide Numbers**. (See 26a)

7 **Save**.

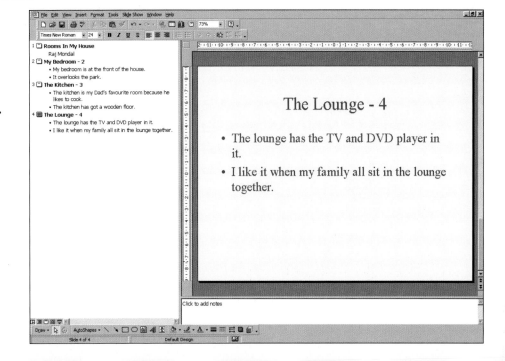

Adding a Design Template

1 Click **Format**.

2 Click **Apply Design Template**.

3 Click a **Design**.

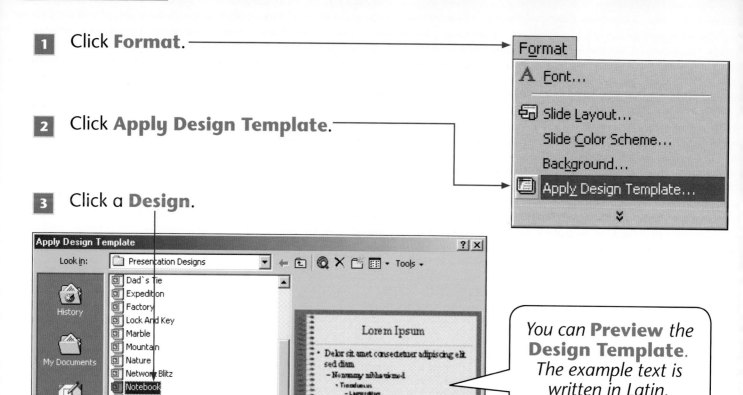

You can **Preview** the **Design Template**. The example text is written in Latin.

4 Click **Apply**.

PowerPointWorks

1 Open a **New Blank Presentation**.

2 Apply your favourite **Design Template** to the presentation. (See 28a)

3 Create a **Title Slide**, 'Places I Have Visited'.

4 Create a series of three **Slides**, each describing a place that you have visited.

Include sentences about:

- The name of the place
- What you saw
- What you liked about it.

Places I Have Visited

By Ananda Mondal

Blackpool

- I went to Blackpool to visit my Grandma.
- We went to Blackpool Pleasure Beach and I had a ride on the Big One.
- I went to the top of Blackpool Tower.
- I had a donkey ride.

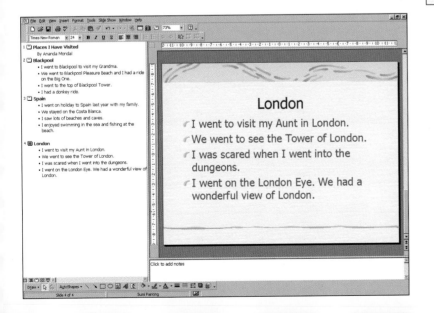

London

- I went to visit my Aunt in London.
- We went to see the Tower of London.
- I was scared when I went into the dungeons.
- I went on the London Eye. We had a wonderful view of London.

5 **Save**.

Working in the Outline Pane

You can read what is on each slide in the **Outline Pane**.

Adding Text in the Outline Pane

1 **Open** an existing presentation.

2 Move the cursor to where you want to add text.

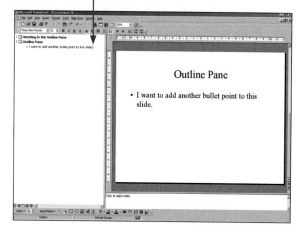

3 Type your text.

> **Remember**
> *Text in objects does not show in the* **Outline Pane**.

Adding a New Slide in the Outline Pane

3 Click the title of the slide you want your **New Slide** to follow.

4 Click **Insert**.

5 Click **New Slide**.

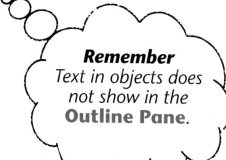

6 Click an **AutoLayout**.

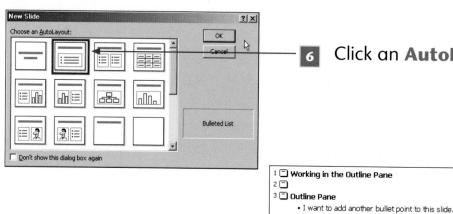

> *I have inserted a* **New Slide** *after* **Slide 1**.

PowerPointWorks

APPLICATION

1 **Open** your 'At the Farm' presentation.

2 Apply a **Design Template** to the presentation. (See 28a)

3 Add two more animals to your list in the **Outline Pane**. (See 29a)

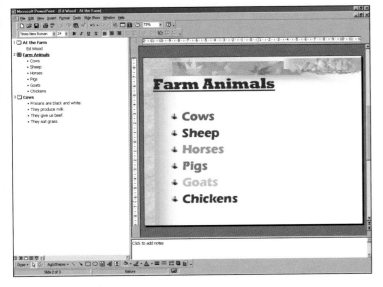

4 Insert a **New Slide (Bulleted List)** between **Slides 2** and **3**.

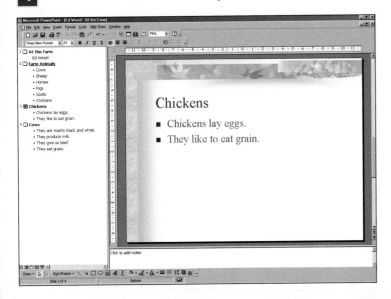

5 Type a few sentences about one of the new animals.

6 **Save**.

Changing the Slide Order

You can rearrange the slides in your presentation in two different ways.

1 Click the **Slide Sorter View** icon in the bottom left corner of the **Outline Pane**.

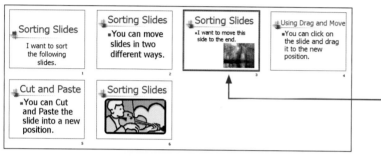

2 Click and hold the **Slide** that you want to move.

3 Drag the **Slide** to its new position.

OR

Slide Sorter View

4 Click the **Slide Sorter View** icon.

5 Click the **Slide** that you want to move.

6 Click **Edit**.

7 Click **Cut**.

8 Click where you want the **Slide** to be placed.

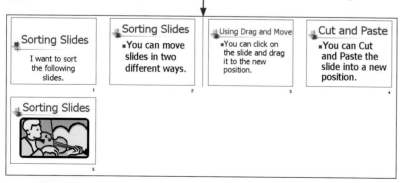

9 Click **Edit**.

10 Click **Paste**.

*You can use **Cut** and **Paste** to change the **Slide Order** in the **Outline Pane** too.*

PowerPointWorks

Rating the Places I Have Visited

SKILL: Changing the Slide Order

APPLICATION

1 **Open** your 'Places I Have Visited' presentation.

2 Rate the places you visited using the **5-Point Star AutoShape**.

> Use a five-star scale:
>
> ***** = Favourite
>
> * = Least favourite.

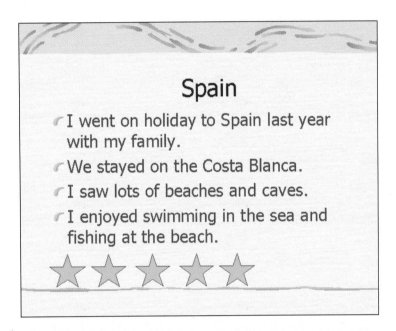

3 Change the **Slide Order** of your presentation so that your least favourite place is shown after the title slide. (See 30a)

4 Your second favourite place should appear next and your favourite place should come last.

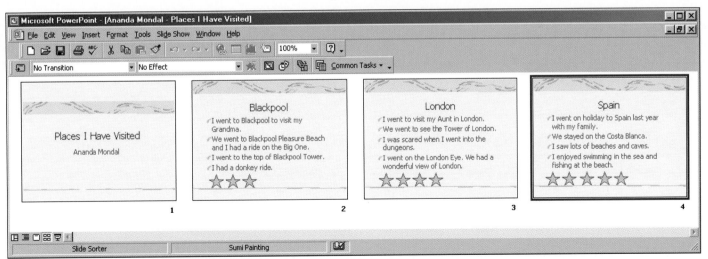

5 **Save**.

PowerPointWorks

31

SKILL & APPLICATION

1 Open a **New Blank Presentation**.

2 Create a **Title Slide** called 'Me and My Friends' and add your name as the subtitle.

3 Insert a **New Slide (Chart)**.

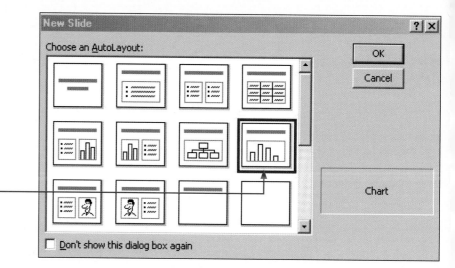

4 Add the title, 'Height of My Friends'.

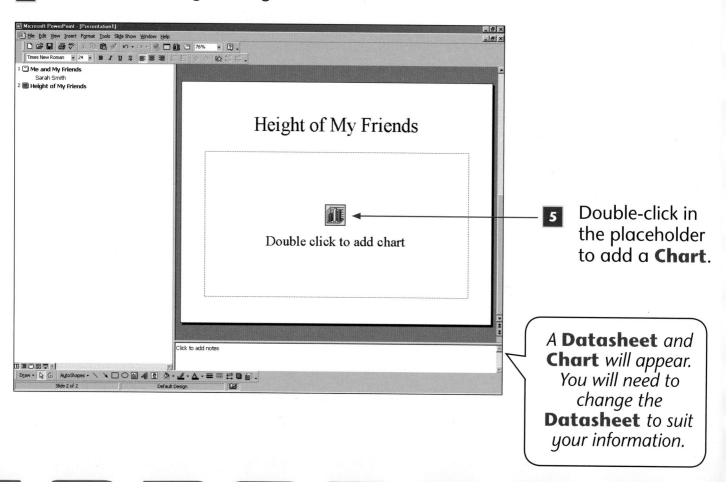

5 Double-click in the placeholder to add a **Chart**.

*A **Datasheet** and **Chart** will appear. You will need to change the **Datasheet** to suit your information.*

6 Click the **Cell** containing the 'East' **Row** heading and type 'Height in cm'.

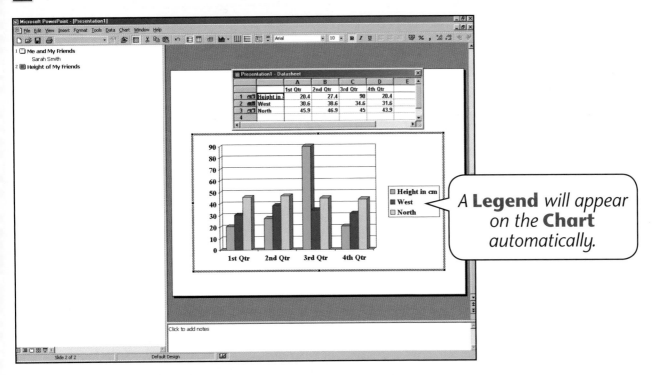

*A **Legend** will appear on the **Chart** automatically.*

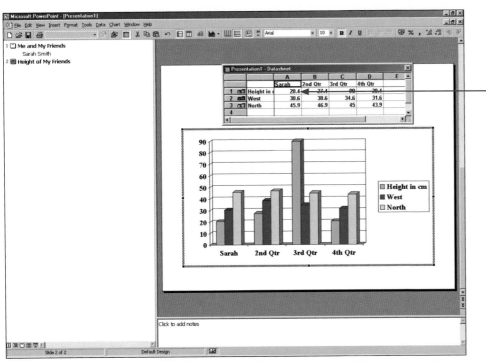

7 Click the **Cell** containing the **Column A** title, '1st Qtr', and type your name.

8 Add the names of four of your friends as titles in **Columns B, C, D** and **E**.

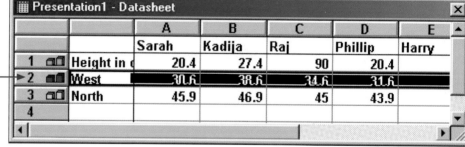

You now need to delete the information in **Rows 2** and **3**. To do this:

9 Click the grey rectangle at the beginning of **Row 2** to select everything in the **Row**.

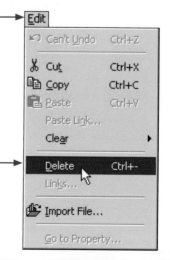

Presentation1 - Datasheet

		A	B	C	D	E
		Sarah	Kadija	Raj	Phillip	Harry
1	Height in c	20.4	27.4	90	20.4	
2	West	30.6	38.6	34.6	31.6	
3	North	45.9	46.9	45	43.9	
4						

10 Click **Edit**.

Edit

↶ Can't Undo	Ctrl+Z
✂ Cut	Ctrl+X
▤ Copy	Ctrl+C
▦ Paste	Ctrl+V
Paste Link...	
Clear	▶
Delete	Ctrl+-
Links...	
▣ Import File...	
Go to Property...	

11 Click **Delete**.

12 **Delete** the contents of **Row 3**.

Adding Charts (continued)

13 Click **Cell A1** and type your height. Add the heights of your four friends.

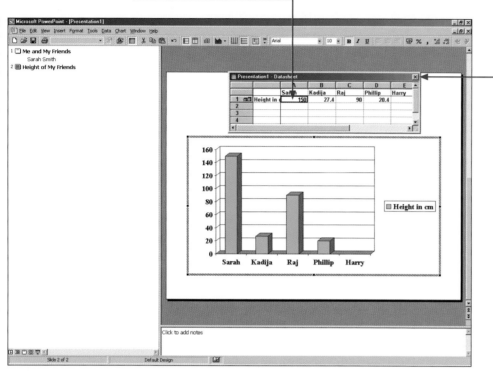

14 Click ✖ to **Close** the **Datasheet**.

Now create another **Chart** to practise this skill.

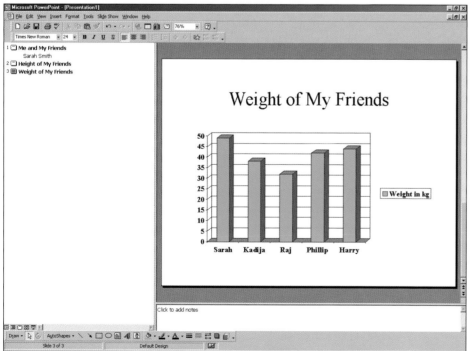

15 Create a **New Slide** (**Chart**), 'Weight of My Friends'.

16 Create a **Chart** showing the weight of your friends.

17 **Save**.

32a

SKILL

There are a variety of **Chart Types** available.

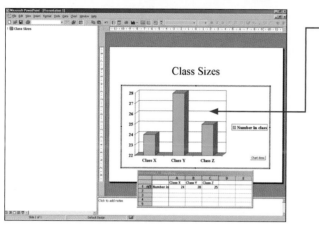

1 Double-click the **Chart** to highlight the outline.
The **Chart** menu will now appear.

2 Click **Chart**.

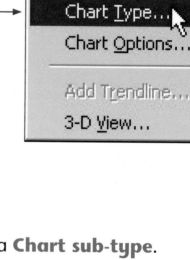

3 Click **Chart Type**.

4 Click the **Standard Types** tab.

5 Click a **Chart Type**.

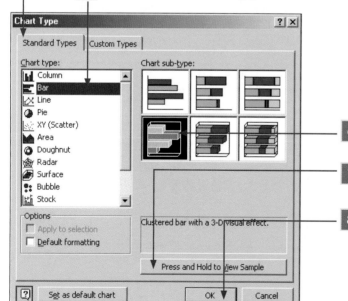

6 Click a **Chart sub-type**.

7 Click and hold to **View Sample Chart**.

8 Click **OK**.

Your **Chart** will change automatically to the new **Chart Type** you have chosen.

Choose a Chart Type

SKILL: Changing the Chart Type

APPLICATION

You need to choose the best **Chart** to suit your information.

1 **Open** your 'Me and My Friends' presentation.

2 Move to the 'Weight of My Friends' slide.

3 Try changing the **Chart** to different **Chart Types**. (See 32a)

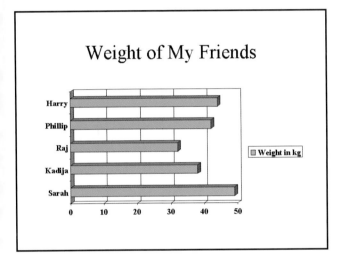

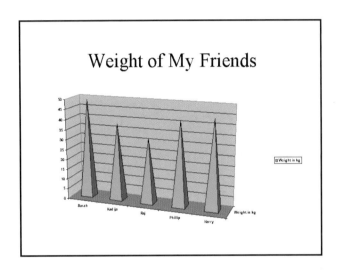

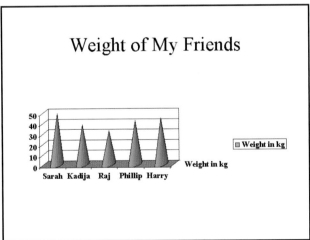

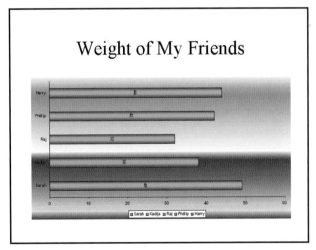

*You can find a wider selection of **Charts** by clicking the **Custom Charts** tab.*

4 **Save**.

33a

SKILL

You can change the **Layout** of your slide.

1 Click **Format**.

2 Click **Slide Layout**.

Changing the Slide Layout

- I want to change the layout of this slide.
- I want to be able to add ClipArt.

3 Click a new layout.

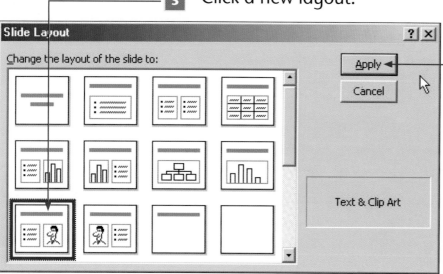

4 Click **Apply**.

Remember
*You should change
the **Slide Layout**
to one that suits
the content of
the slide.*

Changing the Slide Layout

- I have changed the layout of this slide.
- I have added ClipArt.

Add Descriptions to Charts

SKILL: Changing the Slide Layout

APPLICATION

1 **Open** your 'Me and My Friends' presentation.

2 Select the 'Height of My Friends' slide.

3 Change the **Slide Layout** to **Text & Chart** or **Chart & Text**. (See 33a)

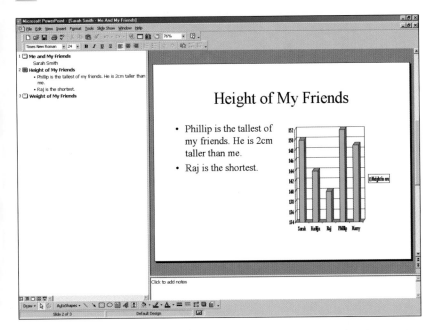

*You can now add comments about the information in the **Chart**.*

4 Repeat this process to change the appearance and content of your 'Weight of My Friends' slide.

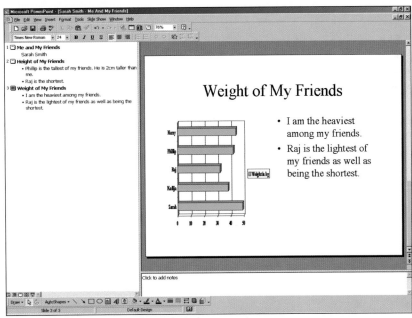

5 **Save**.

Adding Transitions

A **Transition** is used during a **Slide Show** to move from one slide to another. **Transitions** can make your presentation visually attractive.

1 **Open** an existing presentation to which you want to apply a **Transition**.

2 Click **Slide Show**.

3 Click **Slide Transition**.

4 Click the down arrow to find an **Effect**.

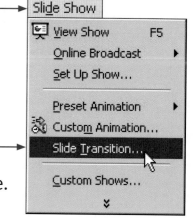

5 Click a **Transition** of your choice.

6 Click **Apply to All**.

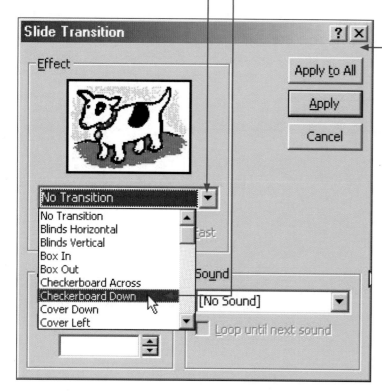

If you want to apply different **Transitions** to individual slides:

● Move to the slide.
● Go back to **2**.
● Click **Apply** instead of **Apply to All**.

*Adding **Transitions** will not change the look of your presentation unless you view it in the **Slide Show View**.*

PowerPointWorks

1 **Open** your 'Places I Have Visited' presentation.

2 Apply a new **Design Template**. (See 28a)

3 Select the **Title Slide** and add a **Transition** of your choice. (See 34a)

I saw lots of beaches and caves.

I enjoyed swimming in the sea and fishing at the beach.

Ananda Mondal

4 Apply a different **Transition** to each slide.

This demonstrates a **Cover Down Transition**.

5 **Save**.

Adding Animation

Adding **Animation** to your presentation allows you to present a **Slide Show** with movements of the objects.

1 **Open** an existing presentation that contains objects that you want to **Animate**.

2 Click the **Text Box** that you want to **Animate**.

> **Text Boxes, Charts, Tables** *and* **ClipArt** *are all* **Objects**.

3 Click **Slide Show**.

> *These are the* **Animation** *types available.*

4 Move to **Preset Animation**.

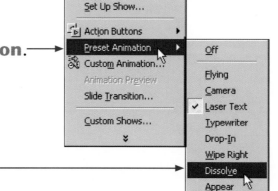

5 Click an **Animation**.

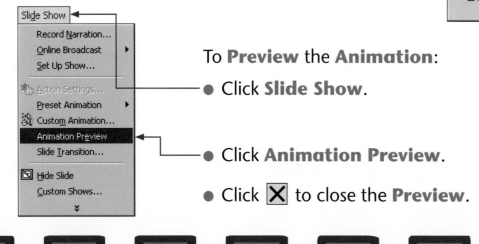

To **Preview** the **Animation**:

● Click **Slide Show**.

● Click **Animation Preview**.

● Click ⊠ to close the **Preview**.

SKILL: Adding Animation

1 Open a **New Blank Presentation**.

2 Create a **Title Slide** called 'A Pet I Know'.

3 Create a presentation about a pet (or pets) you know.

Include slides that describe:
- Type of pet
- Weight
- Food eaten.

4 Apply a **Colour Scheme** to the slides. (See 27a)

This demonstrates the **Fly From Bottom-Left Animation**.

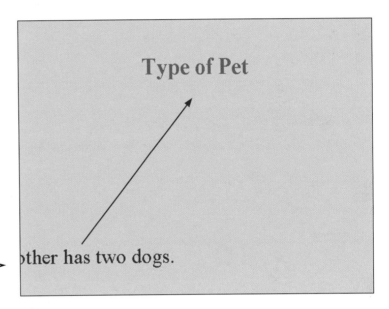

Type of Pet

...ther has two dogs.

5 Add **Transitions** and **Animations** to each of the slides. (See 34a and 35a)

Type of Pet

- My grandmother has two dogs.
- Their names are Suzie and Fluffy.

This demonstrates the **Fly From Bottom Animation**.

- Both dogs are poodles

6 **Save**.

Adding Sounds to Animation

1 **Open** an existing presentation containing animated **Objects**.

2 Click the animated **Object** to which you want to add a **Sound**.

3 Click **Slide Show**.

4 Click **Custom Animation**.

5 Click the **Effects** tab.

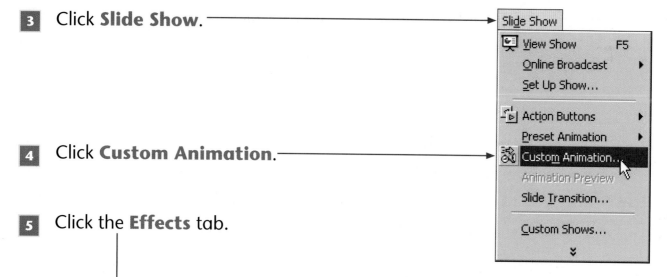

Slide Show

View Show	F5
Online Broadcast	▶
Set Up Show...	
Action Buttons	▶
Preset Animation	▶
Custom Animation...	
Animation Preview	
Slide Transition...	
Custom Shows...	

6 Click the down arrow to view the **Sounds**.

7 Click a **Sound**.

8 Click **Preview** to see and hear the **Effect**.

9 Click **OK**.

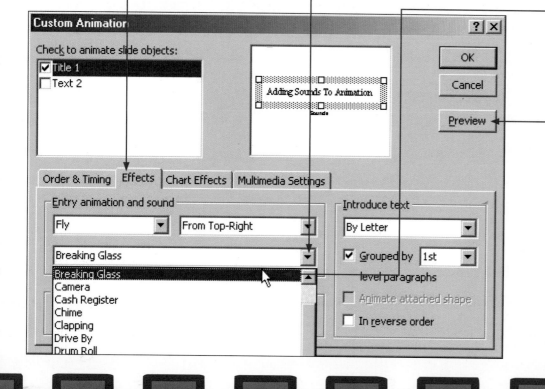

Custom Animation

Check to animate slide objects:
- ☑ Title 1
- ☐ Text 2

Adding Sounds To Animation

OK
Cancel
Preview

Order & Timing | Effects | Chart Effects | Multimedia Settings

Entry animation and sound

Fly | From Top-Right

Breaking Glass

- Breaking Glass
- Camera
- Cash Register
- Chime
- Clapping
- Drive By
- Drum Roll

Introduce text

By Letter

☑ Grouped by 1st
level paragraphs

☐ Animate attached shape

☐ In reverse order

Add Sounds to 'Pets'

SKILL: Adding Sounds to Animation

1 **Open** your 'A Pet I Know' presentation.

2 Find out from where in the world the pet originates and add this information on a **New Slide** (**Bulleted List**).

3 Add a slide that includes **ClipArt** of the pet.

> ## The Origin of the Poodle
>
> • The poodle originates from France.

4 Add **Animation** to each of the slides. (See 35a)

5 Add a **Sound** to each of the **Animations**. (See 36a)

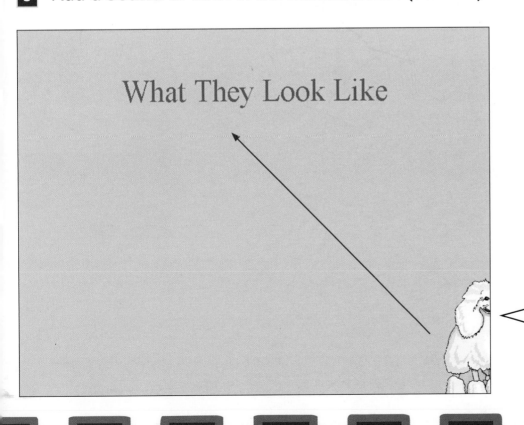

6 **Save**.

> This demonstrates the **Fly From Bottom-Right Animation**.

Adding Custom Animation and After Animation Effects

Custom Animation allows you to choose exactly how your **Objects** move on the screen.
After Animation Effects allow you to change the way your **Objects** appear after they have moved on the screen.

1 **Open** an existing presentation to which you want to add **Custom Animation**.

2 Click the **Object** that you want to **Animate**.

3 Click **Slide Show**.

4 Click **Custom Animation**.

5 Click the **Effects** tab.

6 Click an **Animation**.

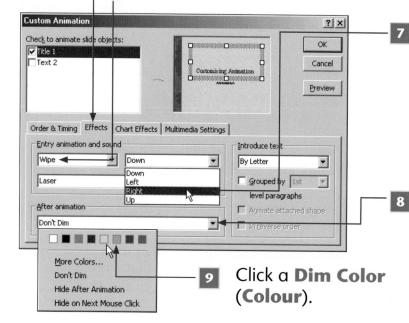

7 Click an **Entry**.

Remember
*You can **Preview** your **Custom Animation**.*

8 Click the **After Animation** arrow.

If you add an After Animation Effect to the last Object to appear on your slide, you will not see it. You will move to the next slide before you can see it.

9 Click a **Dim Color** (**Colour**).

10 Click **OK**.

A Pet You Would Like to Have

SKILL: Adding Custom Animation and After Animation Effects

1 **Open** your 'A Pet I Know' presentation.

2 Add a slide that describes an animal that you would like to have as a pet.

> - Include why you like it.
> - Add any information that you know about it.
> - Add **ClipArt** of the animal.

3 Work through each of the previous slides and add a **Dim Effect** after each **Animation**. (See 37a)

4 Add **Custom Animation** to the new slide.

5 **Save**.

38a SKILL

1. **Open** an existing presentation that contains a **Chart**.

2. Click the **Chart** that you want to **Animate**.

3. Click **Slide Show**.

4. Click **Custom Animation**.

5. Click the **Chart Effects** tab.

6. Click the arrow to show the **Introduce Chart Elements** options.

7. Select the order in which you want the **Chart Elements** to appear.

8. Click an **Effect**.

9. Click a **Sound**.

10. Click **OK**.

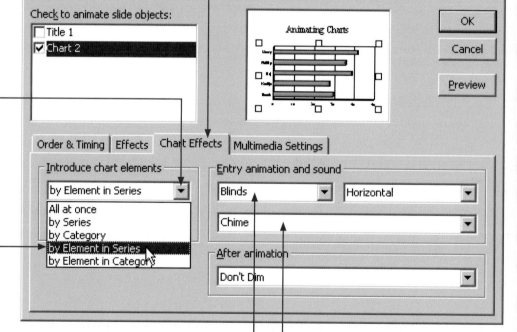

Remember *You can* **Preview** *your* **Chart Animation**.

1 **Open** your 'Me and My Friends' presentation.

2 Add **Chart Animation** to the 'Height of My Friends' **Chart**. (See 38a)

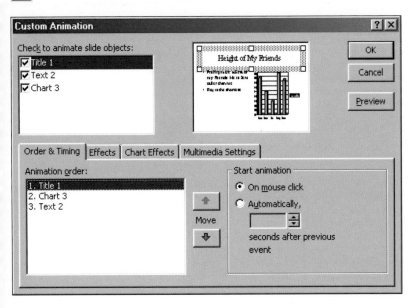

3 Add **Chart Animation** to the 'Weight of My Friends' **Chart**.

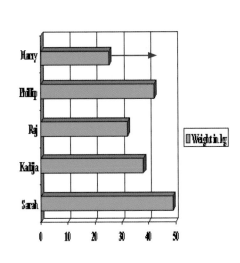

Weight of My Friends

- I am the heaviest among my friends.
- Raj is the lightest of my friends as well as being the shortest.

*This demonstrates the **Wipe Right by Element in Series Animation**.*

4 **Save**.

When you view a **Slide Show** you might find that some **Animated Objects** do not appear in the **Order** you want them to. You can change the **Animation Order** to suit your presentation.

1 Click the **Slide** whose **Animation Order** you want to set.

2 Click **Slide Show**.

3 Click **Custom Animation**.

4 Click the **Order & Timing** tab.

5 Click the **Object** that you want to appear at different time.

Slide Show	
🖳 View Show	F5
Online Broadcast	▶
Set Up Show...	
🔄 Action Buttons	▶
Preset Animation	▶
🐾 Custom Animation...	
Animation Preview	
Slide Transition...	
Custom Shows...	
✖	

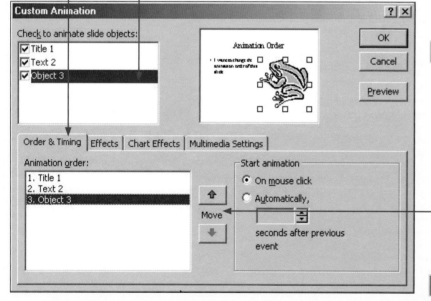

6 Click the **Move Up** or **Move Down** arrows to change the **Order** in which the **Object** appears.

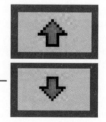

7 Click **OK**.

Check your **Animation Order** has changed.

The Tallest and Lightest

SKILL: Setting the Animation Order

1 **Open** your 'Me and My Friends' presentation.

2 Add **Animation** to the title and the text that describes the weight chart. (See 35a)

3 Change the **Order** of the **Animation** so that the title appears first, then the chart and then the text. (See 39a)

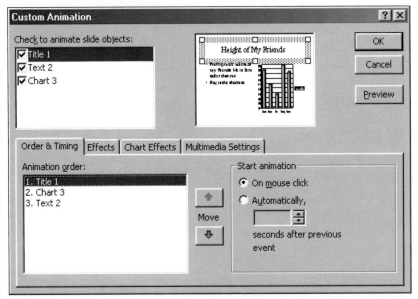

4 Add **Animation** to the title and the text that describes the weight chart.

5 Change the **Order** of the **Animation** so that the title comes first then the chart and then the text.

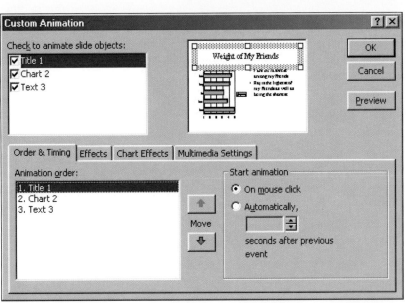

6 **Save**.

Setting the Timings between Animations

1 Click the **Slide** on which you want to set the **Animation Timing**.

2 Click **Slide Show**.

3 Click **Custom Animation**.

4 Click the **Order & Timing** tab.

5 Click the **Object** whose **Timing** you want to set.

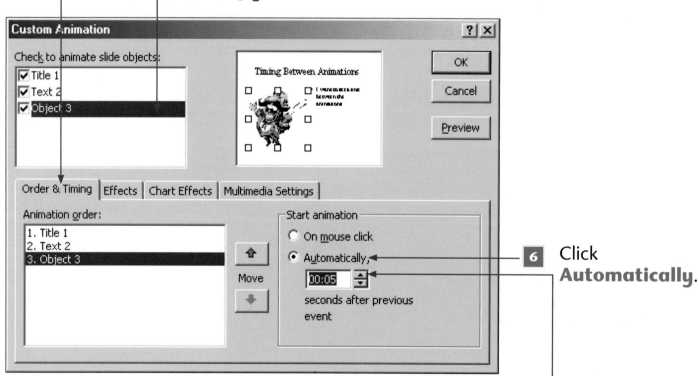

6 Click **Automatically**.

7 Click the up arrow to increase the amount of time before the **Animation**.

8 Click **OK**.

My Ideal Job

SKILL: Setting the Timings between Animations

1 Create a **New Presentation**, 'My Ideal Job'.

2 Include slides for each of the following categories.

- The title of the job
- What the job involves
- What qualifications you need
- Why you would like to do it.

3 Change the **Font** and apply a **Design Template** to all the slides.

4 **Animate** the titles and the text.

My Ideal Job

Suma Mondal

Teaching

- There are many different forms of teaching.
- Teaching involves training others in new skills and subjects.
- Teaching is a job that requires dedication.
- Teaching is a worthwhile job that has many rewards.

Why I Want to Be a Teacher

- I would like to be a teacher because it would involve working with children.
- I would be helping others to learn new subjects.
- I would like to work in a primary school with 7-11 year olds.
- I would specialise in English.

---

5 Set the **Timing** between the title and the text **Animation** on each slide. (See 40a)

6 **Save**.

Viewing your Slide Show and Removing Animation

41a **SKILL**

You can **View** your **Slide Show** in two different ways.

Viewing your Slide Show

1 Click **Slide Show**. ─────────────────────────────►

2 Click **View Show**.───────────────

Slide Show menu:
- View Show   F5
- Record Narration...
- Online Broadcast ▶
- Set Up Show...
- Action Settings...
- Preset Animation ▶
- Custom Animation...
- Slide Transition...
- Hide Slide
- Custom Shows...

Menu (right-click):
- Next
- Previous
- Go ▶
- Meeting Minder...
- Speaker Notes
- Pointer Options ▶
- Screen ▶
- Help
- End Show

3 Click the mouse button to move through the **Slides**.

4 If you want to end the **Slide Show** at any time, click the right mouse button.

5 Click **End Show**.

> *You can **View** a **Slide Show** by clicking the **Slide Show** icon in the bottom left corner of your screen.*

Slide Show

Removing Animation

You might find that after you have seen your presentation, you might want to remove some **Animation**.

6 Click **Slide Show**.

7 Click **Custom Animation**.

8 Click the box to remove the tick. The **Object** will no longer be **Animated**.

9 Click **OK**.

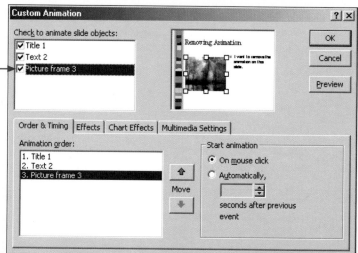

1 Create a **New Presentation** about a European country.

2 Include a slide for each of the following categories.

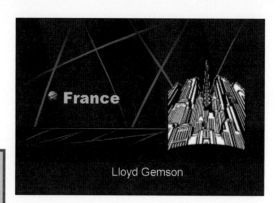

- Location
- Population, area, capital city, languages spoken
- Interesting places to visit.

3 Change the **Font** and apply a **Design Template**.

4 **Animate** the titles and the text.

5 Set the **Timing** between the appearance of the title and the text **Animation**. (See 40a)

Places To Visit

- Eiffel Tower – Paris
- Louvre – Paris
- The Palace Of Versailles
- Have a ride on the Paris Metro.
- Notre Dame Cathedral.

6 **View** your **Slide Show**. (See 41a)

7 Change any **Animation** that is not appropriate.

8 **Save**.

Adding and Editing Speaker Notes

You can add **Speaker Notes** to help you remember what you want to talk about. You can **Print** them or read them from the screen.

1 Click the **Slide** to which you want to add **Notes**.

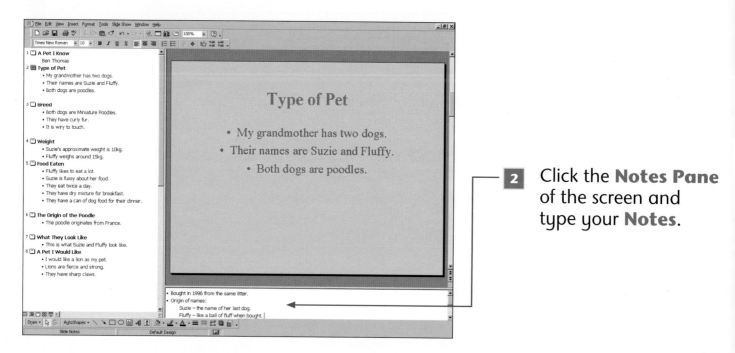

2 Click the **Notes Pane** of the screen and type your **Notes**.

3 If you want to change any of your **Notes** while you are viewing the **Slide Show**, click the right mouse button.

4 Click **Speaker Notes**.

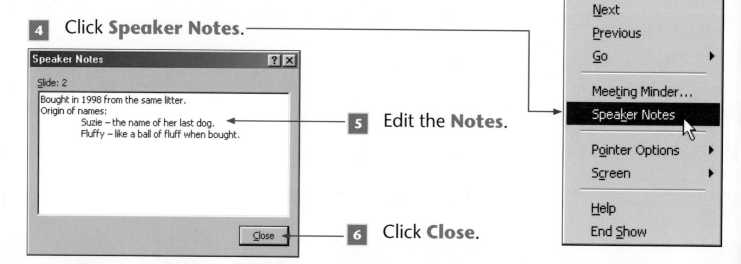

5 Edit the **Notes**.

6 Click **Close**.

A Place of Interest

SKILL: Adding and Editing Speaker Notes

Prepare a presentation about a place that you think will be of interest to your audience.

1 Create a **New** presentation about the place of interest.

2 Insert several slides that describe the place of interest. For example, you might include:

- Location
- Who designed and built it
- Historical background
- What there is to see
- Details of opening times and costs.

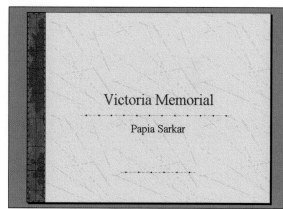

3 Apply a **Design Template**.

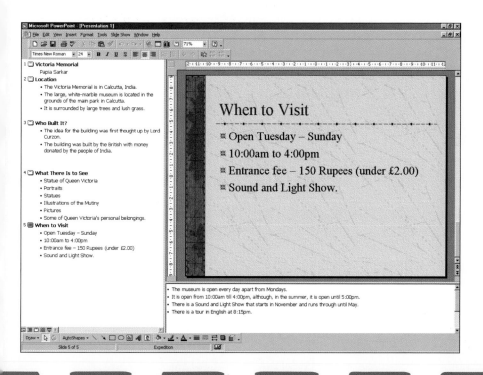

4 **Animate** the titles and the text.

5 Set a time between the title and the text **Animation**. (See 40a)

6 Add **Speaker Notes** for each of the slides. (See 42a)

7 **Save**.

8 View the **Slide Show**. (See 41a)

© Folens (non-copiable) PowerPointWorks 89

Creating a Summary Slide

1 **Open** an existing presentation.

2 Click the **Slide Sorter View** icon.

Slide Sorter View

3 Select the slides that you want to include in your **Summary**. To select more than one slide, hold down the **Ctrl** key and click the slides you want.

4 Click the **Summary Slide** icon.

Summary Slide

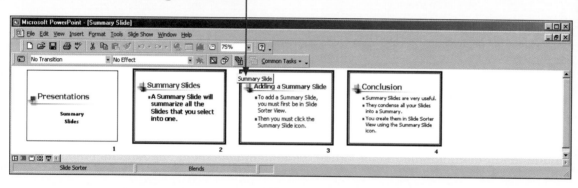

The new **Summary Slide** will appear in front of the slides you select to be summarised.

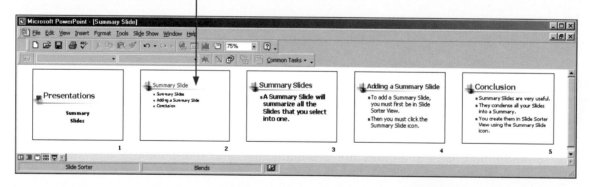

*If you want to change the position of the slide in the presentation, you can drag the **Summary** slide to a new location. (See 30a)*

Summary Slide

- Summary Slides
- Adding a Summary Slide
- Conclusion

About Me – A Summary

SKILL: Creating a Summary Slide

1 **Open** your 'About Me' presentation.

2 Add **Animation** to the slides.

3 Set a time between the title and the text **Animation**.

4 Create a **Summary Slide** of the presentation. (See 43a)

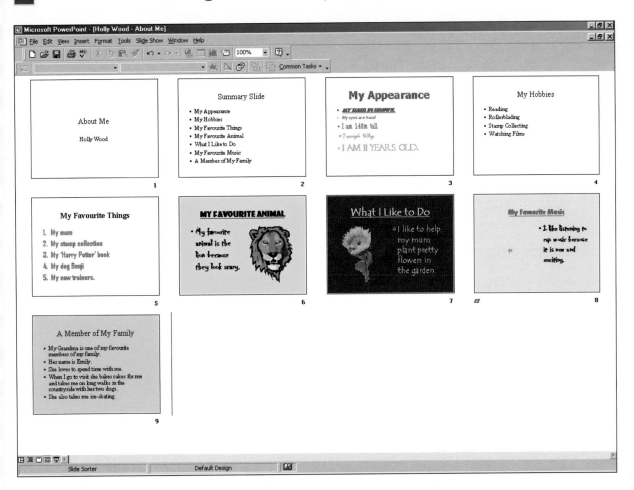

5 Add **Speaker Notes** for each of the slides. (See 42a)

6 **Save**.

7 **View** the **Slide Show**. (See 41a)

44a

SKILL

You can **View** your presentation, as the audience will see it, to make sure you are happy with it.

1 **Open** an existing presentation.

2 Click **Slide Show**.

3 Click **View Show**. The **Title Slide** of your presentation will appear first.

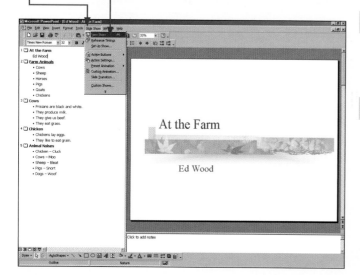

4 Click the **Menu** button (in the bottom left of your screen).

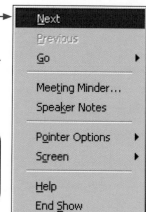

5 Click **Next**. The next slide in the sequence will appear on the screen.

*The **Slide Navigator** lists all the slides in your presentation.*

OR

6 Click **Go**, if you want to move to a particular slide.

*You can view your **Speaker Notes**, if you wish.*

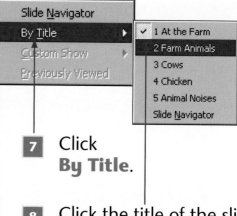

7 Click **By Title**.

8 Click the title of the slide you want to **View**.

Wild Animals

SKILL: Navigating a Slide Show

1 Create a **New Presentation** about a wild animal.

2 Add **Transitions** between the slides. (See 34a)

3 Add **Animation** to the slides.

4 Set the time between the title and the text **Animation**.

5 Create a **Summary Slide** of the presentation. (See 43a)

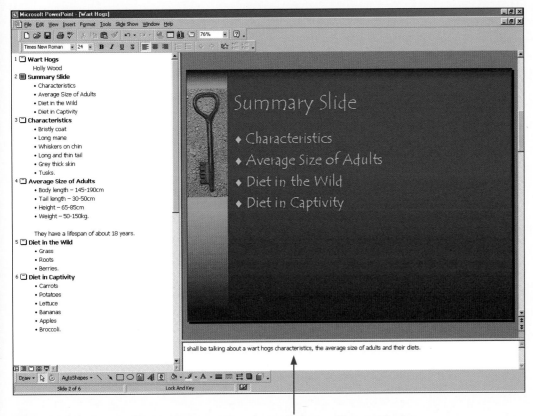

You might include these slides in your presentation.

6 Add **Speaker Notes** to the slides. (See 42a)

7 Check the presentation in **Slide Show View** using the **Slide Navigator**. (See 44a)

8 **Save**.

PowerPointWorks

Adding a Pointer

Adding a **Pointer** to your presentation enables you to point to important aspects of the slide.

1 **Open** an existing presentation.

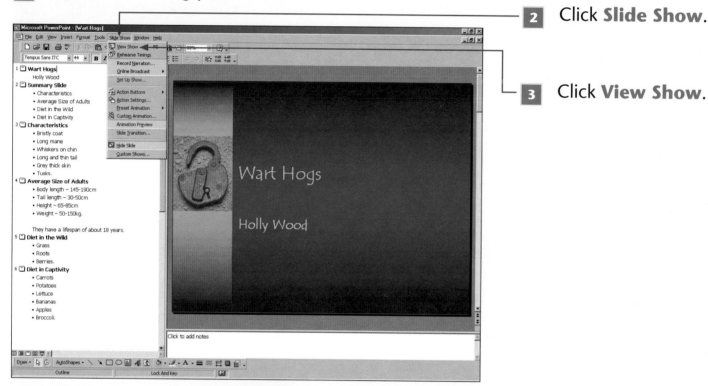

2 Click **Slide Show**.

3 Click **View Show**.

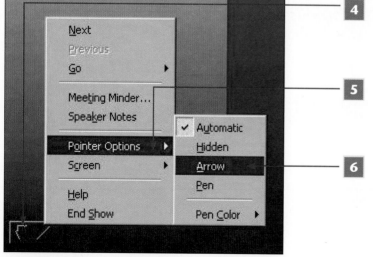

4 Click the **Menu** button.

5 Move to **Pointer Options**.

6 Click a **Pointer Option**.

The **Pointer** will appear on the screen.

PowerPointWorks

© Folens (non-copiable)

1 Create a **New** presentation, 'The Use of Computers at our School'.

2 You might include slides about:

- Location of computers
- Use of computers
- Who uses the computers
- Computer Suite timetable.

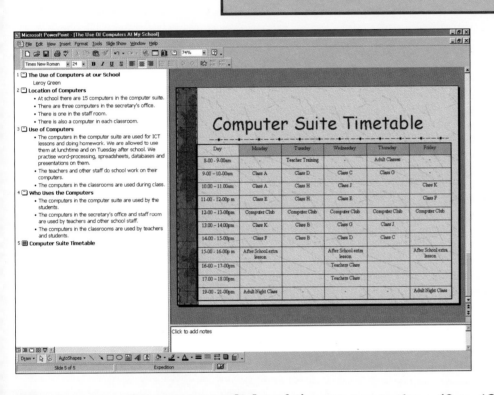

3 Add **Transitions** between the slides.

4 Add **Animation** to the slides.

5 Set the time between the title and the text **Animation**.

6 Create a **Summary Slide** of the presentation. (See 43a)

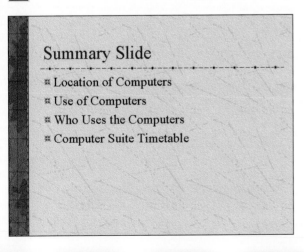

7 **Save**.

8 Start the presentation and right-click the mouse to **Navigate**. (See 44a)

9 Add a **Pointer**, so you can point to different parts of the Computer Suite timetable. (See 45a)

During the presentation, you can draw the audience's attention to particular points with the **Pen Pointer**.

1 **Open** an existing presentation.

2 Click **Slide Show**.

3 Click **View Show**.

4 Click the **Menu** button.

Next
Previous
Go
Meeting Minder...
Speaker Notes
Pointer Options
Screen
Help
End Show

✓ Automatic
Hidden
Arrow
Pen
Pen Color

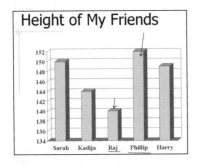

5 Move to **Pointer Options**.

6 Click **Pen**.

Changing the Pen Colour

7 Click **Pointer Options**.

8 Click **Pen Color** (**Colour**).

✓ Automatic
Hidden
Arrow
Pen
Pen Color

Black
White
Red
Green
Blue
Cyan
Magenta
Yellow
Grey
Reset

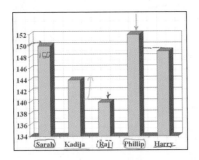

9 Click the **Pen Color** (**Colour**) of your choice.

You can clear your **Pen** marks from the **Slide Show**.

10 Click the **Menu** button.

Next
Previous
Go
Meeting Minder...
Speaker Notes
Pointer Options
Screen
Help
End Show

Pause
Black Screen
Erase Pen

12 Click **Erase Pen**.

11 Click **Screen**.

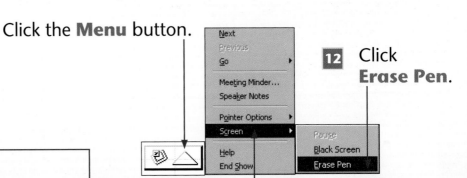

What I Ate Yesterday

SKILL: Using the Pen Pointer

1 Create a **New** presentation, 'What I Ate Yesterday'.

2 Insert a different slide for each meal.

> Include:
> - Drinks that contain milk
> - Drinks that contain sugar.

3 If you ate between meals, add a slide for each time you ate, for example, add one called 'Mid-morning Snack'.

4 Add **Transitions** between the slides.

5 Add **Animation** to the slides.

6 Set the time between the title and the **Text Box Animation**.

7 Create a **Summary Slide** of the presentation. (See 43a)

8 View the presentation and use the **Pen** to highlight the different food types. (See 46a)

- Underline proteins in red.
- Add a yellow star next to any sugary foods and drinks.
- Circle fruit and vegetables in green.
- Add a cyan square next to the dairy products.
- Add a magenta triangle next to the carbohydrates.
- Underline fatty foods in grey.

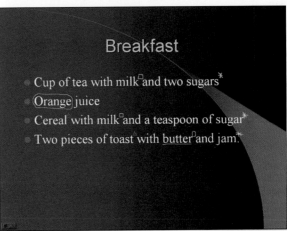

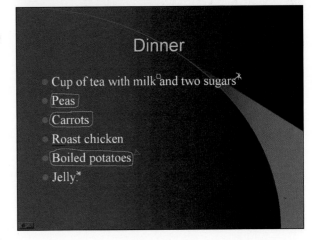

*Think of how you might use the **Pen** when you give a presentation to an audience.*

9 **Save**.

Printing a Presentation

You can **Print** your presentation in four different ways. You can **Print** individual **Slides**, the **Notes** or the **Outline View** of your presentation as well as **Handouts** for your audience.

Slide

Outline View

Handouts

Notes Pages

1 Click **File**.

2 Click **Print**.

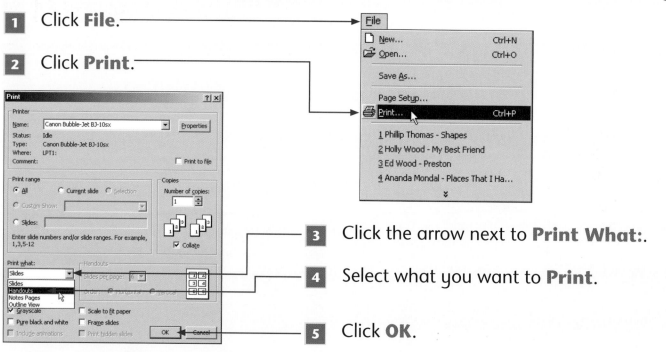

3 Click the arrow next to **Print What:**.

4 Select what you want to **Print**.

5 Click **OK**.

To select the number of slides you want on your **Handouts**:

6 Click how many **Slides per page** you want to **Print**.

7 Click the **Order** in which you want the slides to appear.

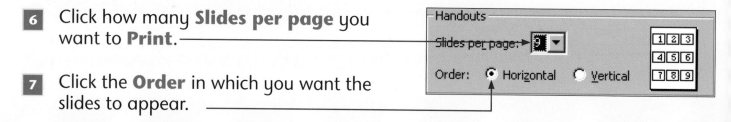

SKILL: Printing a Presentation

47b

APPLICATION

1 **Open** your 'About Me' presentation.

2 Insert a **New Slide**, 'My Favourite Meal'.

3 Type some sentences about your favourite meal.

> ## My Favourite Meal
>
> - My favourite meal is spaghetti bolognese.
> - It is a pasta dish from Italy.
> - The spaghetti is a long thin pasta.
> - The bolognese is a minced beef and tomato mix.

4 Redo the **Summary Slide** so that it includes the new slide.

5 **Print** a **Handout** of the whole presentation with **3 Slides per page**. (See 47a)

> ### Summary Slide
>
> - My Appearance
> - My Hobbies
> - My Favourite Things
> - My Favourite Animal
> - What I Like to Do
> - My Favourite Music
> - A Member of My Family
> - My Favourite Meal

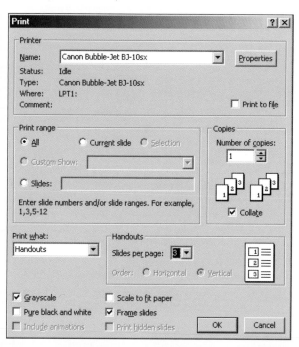

6 **Save**.

7 **Open** your 'My Best Friend' presentation.

8 Add a slide describing your best friend's favourite food, create a **Summary Slide** and **Print Handouts** of the presentation.

Adding a Hyperlink to an Object

Adding a **Hyperlink** to an object allows you to move to another File or another part of your presentation.

1 Right-click the object to which you want to add a **Hyperlink**.

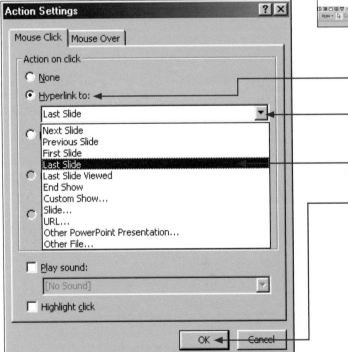

2 Click **Action Settings**.

3 Click **Hyperlink to:**.

4 Click the down arrow.

5 Click a destination.

6 Click **OK**.

When you click your chosen object, the **Hyperlink** *will take you to the* **Last Slide** *in the presentation.*

A different way to add **Hyperlinks**:

● Click **Slide Show**.
● Click **Action Settings**.
● Go back to **3**.

Move from Picture to Picture

SKILL: Adding a Hyperlink to an Object

APPLICATION

1 Open a **New Blank Presentation**.

2 On the **Title Slide**, type your name and class.

3 On four different slides, add **ClipArt** of your choice and type a brief description of each.

4 Apply a **Design Template**.

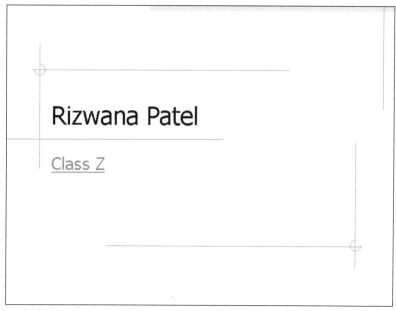

Rizwana Patel

Class Z

Woman with a Dog

◆ The ClipArt shows a woman with a dog. She may be the owner or a vet.

5 Add **Hyperlinks** from each piece of **ClipArt** to the following slide. (See 48a)

6 On the last slide, create a **Hyperlink** from the **ClipArt** back to the **Title Slide**.

*When you view your **Slide Show**, you will be able to click the objects to move around your presentation.*

7 **Save**.

Adding Hyperlinks to Other Presentations

You can add a **Hyperlink** to your slide that will take you to another presentation.

1 Move to the slide to which you want to add the **Hyperlink**.

2 Highlight the text to which you want to add a **Hyperlink**.

3 Right-click the mouse.

4 Click **Action Settings**.

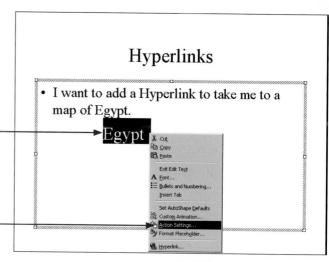

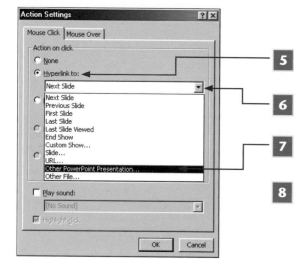

5 Click **Hyperlink to:**.

6 Click the down arrow.

7 Click **Other PowerPoint Presentation**.

8 Find the presentation to which you want to link.

9 Click **OK**.

10 Select the **Slide** from which you want to start.

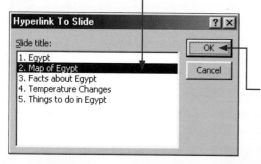

11 Click **OK**.

12 Click **OK** in the **Action Settings** box.

My Family

SKILL: Adding Hyperlinks to Other Presentations

APPLICATION

You are going to create a presentation about a member of your family.

1 Open a **New Blank Presentation**.

2 Create a **Title Slide**.

My Brother Ben

Holly Wood

3 Insert four different slides about the member of your family that you have chosen.

You might include:
- Appearance
- Hobbies
- Favourite Things
- What you would change about them.

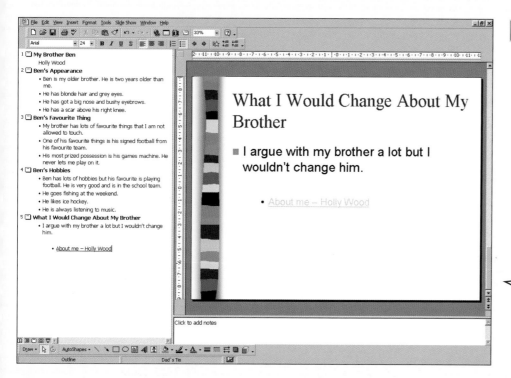

4 Add a **Hyperlink** to your presentation that links to your 'About Me' presentation. (See 49a)

> The **Hyperlink** will be underlined. If you click the **Hyperlink** during the **Slide Show**, it will take you to your 'About Me' presentation.

5 **Save**.

Adding a Hyperlink to a Website

You might want to add a **Hyperlink** to a **Website** so that you can refer to something that can be viewed online.

1 Right-click the object to which you want to add a **Hyperlink**.

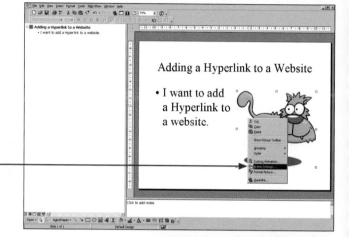

2 Click **Action Settings**.

3 Click **Hyperlink to:**.

4 Click the down arrow.

5 Click **URL**.

6 Type your **Website** address.

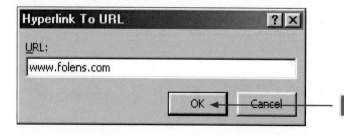

7 Click **OK**.

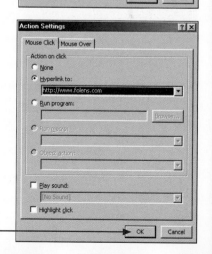

8 Click **OK**.

You will now be able to go to the relevant **Website** by clicking the object.

PowerPointWorks

My Favourite Website

SKILL: Adding a Hyperlink to a Website

50b

APPLICATION

1 Open a **New Blank Presentation**.

2 Add a **Title Slide**, 'My Favourite Website'.

3 Insert a **New Slide** (**Bulleted List**).

4 Type four sentences about why this particular **Website** is your favourite.

5 Apply a **Design Template**.

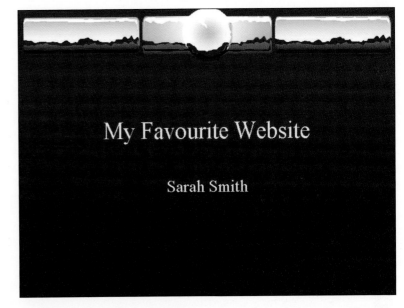

6 Add a **Hyperlink** that links to the **Website**. (See 50a)

Remember Highlight the text to which you want to add a Hyperlink.

The British Museum Website

❖ My favourite website is the British Museum website.

❖ It has information on all the different exhibitions at the museum.

❖ The 'virtual tours' include photos and extra information on the exhibits.

❖ I can use the website to plan my next visit to the museum.

7 **Save**.

Recording Sounds

You can add **Sounds** to your presentation to make it more interesting.

You will need a microphone attached to your computer to record sounds.

1 Click **Insert**.

2 Move to **Movies and Sounds**.

3 Click **Record Sound**.

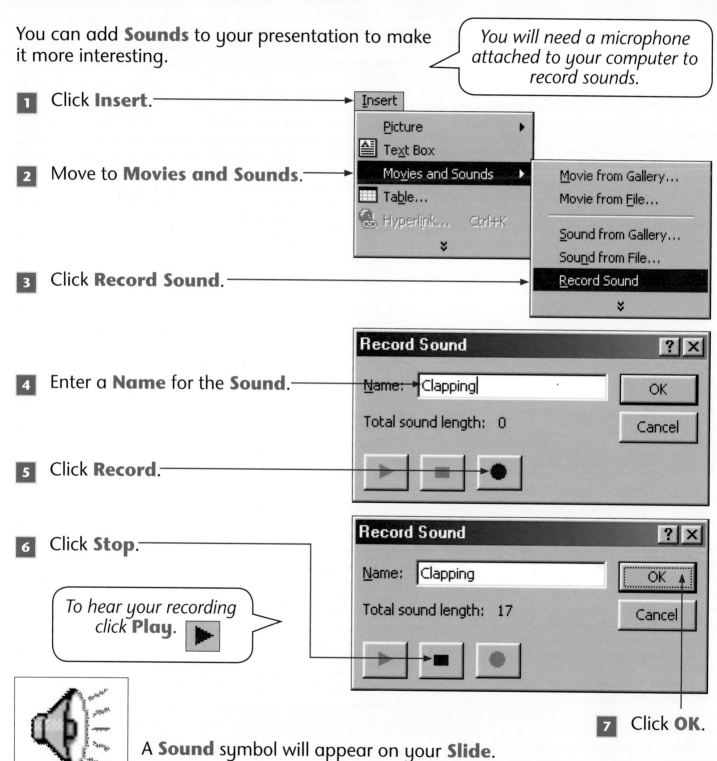

Insert
- Picture ▶
- Te**x**t Box
- Mo**v**ies and Sounds ▶
- Ta**b**le...
- Hyperlink... Ctrl+K

Movies and Sounds submenu:
- Movie from Gallery...
- Movie from File...
- Sound from Gallery...
- Soun**d** from File...
- Record Sound

4 Enter a **Name** for the **Sound**.

Record Sound ? ✕
Name: Clapping
Total sound length: 0
OK
Cancel

5 Click **Record**.

6 Click **Stop**.

*To hear your recording click **Play**.* ▶

Record Sound ? ✕
Name: Clapping
Total sound length: 17
OK
Cancel

7 Click **OK**.

A **Sound** symbol will appear on your **Slide**.

SKILL: Recording sounds

APPLICATION

1 **Open** your 'At the Farm' presentation.

2 Insert a **New Slide**, 'Animal Noises'.

3 List five farm animals and the noises they make.

4 Imitate the sounds of the animals and record them. (See 51a)

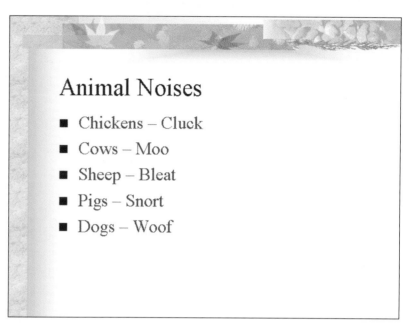

Animal Noises

- Chickens – Cluck
- Cows – Moo
- Sheep – Bleat
- Pigs – Snort
- Dogs – Woof

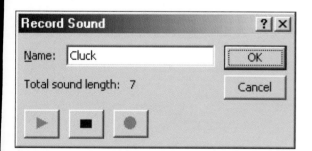

You can record real animals on tape and transfer it to your computer.

Animal Noises

- Chickens – Cluck
- Cows – Moo
- Sheep – Bleat
- Pigs – Snort
- Dogs – Woof

5 View your **Slide Show**.

6 **Print** a handout of the whole presentation with **3 Slides per page**. (See 47a)

7 **Save**.

If you want to do your presentation without worrying about moving to the next slide, you can set the **Timings** so the next slide appears automatically when you want it to.

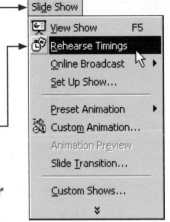

1 Click **Slide Show**.

2 Click **Rehearse Timings**.

3 Run through your **Slide Show** and read what you are going to say about each slide. When you have finished, press **Enter** to move to the next slide.

*You can see your **Timings** in **Slide Sorter View**.*

4 If the **Timing** is suitable, click **Yes**.

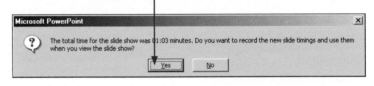

If you already know how long the **Timings** should be:

5 Click the slide whose **Timing** you want to set.

6 Click **Slide Show**.

7 Click **Slide Transition**.

8 Click **Automatically After**.

9 Enter the time (in seconds) after which you want to **Advance** to the next **Slide**.

10 Click **Apply**.

11 Do this for all the **Slides**.

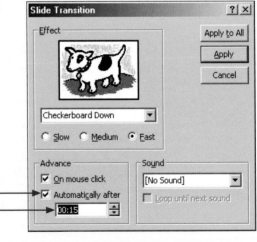

*If you are going to talk about every **Slide** for the same amount of time, click **Apply to All**.*

Fund-raising

Imagine you have been asked to give a presentation to the rest of the school about the fund-raising events your class has organised.

1 Create a presentation, 'Fund-raising for …'.
Name the cause you are supporting.

> You might include slides about:
> - The organisation for which you are fund-raising
> - The good work done by the organisation
> - The fund-raising activities you have organised
> - When and where the activities will take place
> - Details of any costs or tickets that can be purchased.

2 Apply a **Design Template**.

3 Add **Animation** and **Slide Transitions**.

4 **Automate** your presentation.
(See 52a)

5 **Print** a **Handout** of the presentation with **4 Slides per page**. (See 47a)

6 **Save**.

St. Catherine's Hospice

- St Catherine's Hospice is a very caring home for very sick people.
- It is a registered charity.
- It relies on donations from people in the local community.
- Most people in the area know of someone who has been cared for at St Catherine's.

Fund-raising Activity: February

- Matchbox Challenge
- Entry fee of 50p
- 10 prizes
- Entrants to complete the task at home
- Closing date for entries 28th February.

Fund-raising Activity: March

- Design an Easter Bonnet or Hat
- Entry fee of 25p
- 10 Easter Eggs to be won
- Entrants to complete the task at home
- The hats and bonnets will be judged at the Easter Fair.

Adding a Narration

You can add a voice-over to your presentation.
This could be your voice or that of someone else.

1 Click **Slide Show**.

2 Click **Record Narration**.

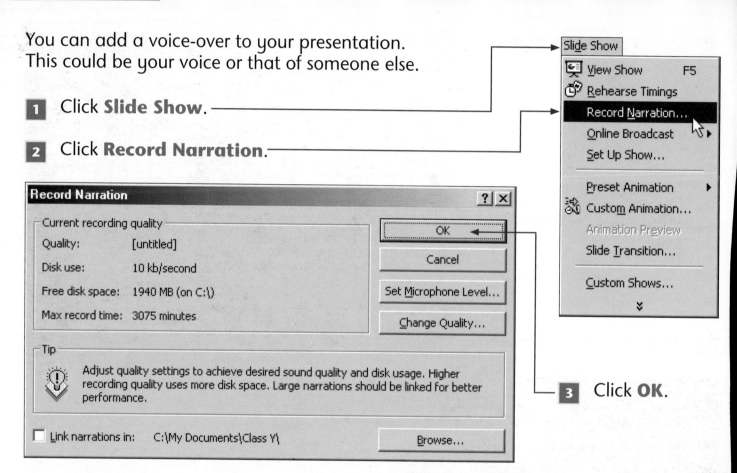

3 Click **OK**.

4 Speak into the microphone while going through the **Slide Show**.
Once you have finished talking about one slide, press the **Enter** key to move
to the next slide.

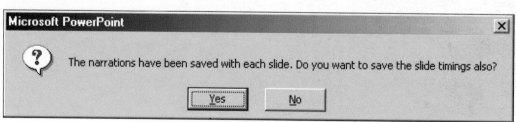

5 Start the **Slide Show** to hear
and see your presentation.

Click **Yes**, *if you want the* **Slide Show** *to
move on at the same pace as you did the*
Narration. *Click* **No**, *if you just want to*
Save the **Narrations**.

PowerPointWorks

Narrate the Fund-raising Presentation

SKILL: Adding a Narration

1 **Open** your 'Fund-raising' presentation.

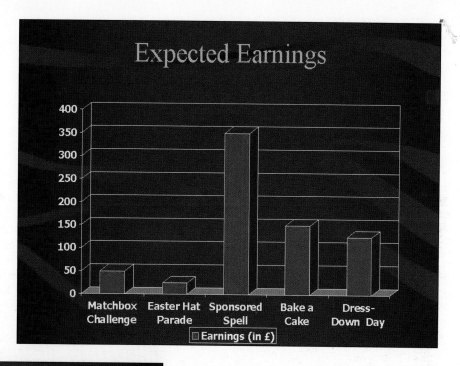

Expected Earnings

Matchbox Challenge   Easter Hat Parade   Sponsored Spell   Bake a Cake   Dress-Down Day

☐ Earnings (in £)

2 Add a **Chart Slide** to show the expected earnings of each event, using a **Bar Chart**. (See 31)

3 Add a **Summary Slide**.

Summary Slide

- St Catherine's Hospice
- Fund-raising Activity: February
- Fund-raising Activity: March
- Fund-raising Activity: April
- Fund-raising Activity: June
- Fund-raising Activity: July
- Expected Earnings

4 Add **Speaker Notes** to the slides.

5 Add a **Narration** to the **Slide Show**. (See 53a)

6 **Print** a **Handout** of the presentation with **6 Slides per page**.

7 **Save**.

Photocopying

Please note that pages from this book may **NOT** be photocopied.

The CLA licence does **NOT** apply to this book.

© 2002 Folens Limited, on behalf of the authors.
United Kingdom: Folens Publishers, Apex Business Centre, Boscombe Road, Dunstable, LU5 4RL.
Email: folens@folens.com

Ireland: Folens Publishers, Greenhills Road, Tallaght, Dublin 24.
Email: info@folens.ie

Poland: JUKA, ul. Renesansowa 38, Warsaw 01-905.

Editor: Emma Thomas
Layout artists: Patricia Hollingsworth
Cover design: Patricia Harrison and Martin Cross

First published 2002 by Folens Limited.
Reprinted 2003.

Screenshots reprinted by permission from Microsoft Corporation.

Microsoft® and PowerPoint® are either registered trademarks or trademarks of Microsoft Corporation in the United States and other countries.

Microsoft PowerPoint software is © 1987–1999 Microsoft Corporation. All rights reserved.

Every effort has been made to trace the copyright holders of material used in this publication. If any copyright holder has been overlooked, we should be pleased to make any necessary arrangements.

British Library Cataloguing in Publication Data. A catalogue record for this publication is available from the British Library.

ISBN 1 84303 142 6